The Women

Yan Lianke

Translated by Jeremy Tiang

VERSO
London • New York

This English-language edition first published by Verso 2026

First published as 她們 (Tamen)

The manufacturer's authorized representative in the EU for product safety (GPSR)
is LOGOS EUROPE, 9 rue Nicolas Poussin, 17000, La Rochelle, France
contact@logoseurope.eu

1 3 5 7 9 10 8 6 4 2

Verso
UK: 6 Meard Street, London W1F 0EG
US: 207 East 32nd Street, New York, NY 10016
versobooks.com

Verso is the imprint of New Left Books

ISBN-13: 978-1-83674-285-2
ISBN-13: 978-1-83674-288-3 (US EBK)
ISBN-13: 978-1-83674-287-6 (UK EBK)

British Library Cataloguing in Publication Data
A catalogue record for this book is available from the British Library

Library of Congress Cataloging-in-Publication Data
A catalog record for this book is available from the Library of Congress

Typeset in Fournier by MJ & N Gavan, Truro, Cornwall
Printed and bound by CPI Group (UK) Ltd, Croydon CR0 4YY

Contents

HUNDRED FLOWERS

In 1956, seven years after his victory in China's Communist Revolution, Mao Zedong extended an invitation to the country's intelligentsia: "Let a hundred flowers bloom, let a hundred different schools of thought contend." As criticism of the Chinese Communist Party swelled, the Hundred Flowers project morphed into something cynical, known as the Anti-Rightist Campaign. As a result, many who had, in good faith, produced texts and essays critical of the party faced repression; many careers were destroyed.

Verso's Hundred Flowers series aims to fulfill Mao's promise in earnest by publishing writing on China from the mainland, the diaspora, and elsewhere. Once a key American ally, China has emerged over the course of this century as the only serious challenger to US global economic hegemony. Yet China remains largely opaque to the West, which is too often ignorant of both the country's history and its contemporary internal dynamics. Books, newspaper articles, and magazine essays abound but at best present simplistic views of China; at worst, these accounts are misleading or scaremongering. Hundred Flowers offers a more nuanced perspective to facilitate serious debate in analyzing China's past, present, and future.

Other titles in this series available from Verso Books:

The Unmaking of the Chinese Working Class by Teemu Ruskola
Involution by the Gonglao Collective, translated by Eli Friedman

Translator's Note

Familial terms in Chinese are complicated, because they are extremely specific. There is no single word for "cousin" but rather different terms depending on whether a cousin is older or younger, male or female, on the father's or mother's side of the family. This poses a challenge to the translator; for instance, the word "biaomei" (表妹), straightforward enough in Chinese, would have to be rendered as "younger female maternal cousin" to capture its full meaning. This is generally too unwieldy to fit neatly into a text, and so choices have to be made. How much of this information is necessary, and how much can be slipped in unobtrusively rather than in a burst of exposition?

Yan Lianke's memoir, being about his family, naturally mentions many of his relatives. Very often, we know someone only as "Third Aunt" without ever finding out her name. And of course, she was not simply an "aunt" in Chinese, but a "gu" (姑), indicating she was the speaker's father's sister; "third" tells us she was the third daughter of her generation. As an added complication, the most senior aunt or uncle has a completely different title, which I have reflected in English by using "Eldest Aunt" or the like, rather than "First Aunt."

I contemplated retaining the original Chinese family terms, perhaps with a glossary, but that seemed to be asking a lot of the reader. In the end, I noticed that there were two main groups of aunts in the book: Yan Lianke's father's sisters, and his father's brothers' wives. The first group I have rendered as "Eldest Aunt," "Second Aunt," and so on, and the second group as "Eldest Aunt-in-Law," "Second Aunt-in-Law," and so on. I trust this will be straightforward enough to follow, but do know that there are many more terms for "uncle" and "aunt" than are represented here.

Preface

Ten Years of Waiting

I had to wait ten years to write this slim volume of essays. I laugh about that, but there's an ache underneath. Imagine a child who wants an apple having to plant a seed, transplant and water the sapling, watch it slowly grow into a fully fledged tree, prune and graft its branches, wait year after year until the day arrives when its crown is suddenly laden with fruit. Only then can he run over and pluck the apple he's spent a decade longing for.

There are times when writing is a process of anguished yearning and waiting.

Ten years ago, when I wrote *Three Brothers*, my friends in publishing kept encouraging me to take advantage of its success and put out a book about the women in my family. I stood my ground and refused to write that book, because I didn't want to write about these women the same way I did about my father and his brothers. In my hometown, women may be people, but on that piece of earth where I come from, they are women first and foremost. Under those roofs, in those courtyards, in those fields, falling into the cracks and crevices of history, they laugh, cry, get married, have children, and grow old—then their daughters walk the same paths they did, or find other well-trodden routes, the same hopes and desires and striving, prospering or declining, numbness or hysteria, crying out or silence. This piece of earth is where they were born, and where they grew old and ended their days. The city is the sunrise of their future, and also the sunset of their passing. Desire can be a sort of strength, but it can also constrain and hold back your destiny.

Random chance decides the inevitable.

Death waits to be born.

The blind pursuit of marriage and sex is both a sort of beginning and also an ending that has lain in wait from the very start.

I have no way of knowing whether womanhood shaped their personhood, or whether their personalities turned them into the sorts of women they were. Their destiny was both a wide open plain and a pit they couldn't escape. They were the same types of people as the men around them. But also completely different. I have a clear understanding of my father and uncles, of myself, of all these men. Yet when it comes to my mother and aunts, my sisters and wife and sister-in-law, my cousins, and all these other women—they are familiar to me, but also strangers.

I couldn't write what I didn't know. Unable to wrap my head around it, I had to wait.

I ended up waiting ten years.

It's not like I attained enlightenment in this time. Rather, the day came when I looked at my village in winter, at the people warming themselves by the fire, and I thought about the night of Jesus's trial, when Peter stood by a fire alongside servants and slaves. When I looked at my mother and sisters smiling or weeping, I thought how other women thousands of miles away were also smiling or weeping at the same moment. Turns out we are not sealed off from the world. Like the two ends of a scale or a seesaw, a movement here causes distant tremors there, or sometimes greater shocks.

The far ends of the world are intimately connected.

With that, I felt able to start writing.

I'd finally seen that when the women were cold here, someone was shivering elsewhere; when they died here, someone far away was silently shedding tears. On the flip side, when a baby was born in a distant place, someone here would be beaming and handing out celebratory red eggs. And when we happened to see the great cross in the western sky, the crucifixion wounds in our hearts opened and blood trickled out.

I began to believe that when a young woman got married at this end, a dove flew through the air on the far side, landing on the holy mother's shoulder. And if we smiled on a wintry day, a tree somewhere else on earth would blossom and put forth fruit.

That's pretty much how it happened.

After ten years of waiting, I suddenly felt ready to write about the women.

So I started work on *The Women*.

I wrote about their tears and laughter, their silences

and frenzies, their quiet suffering and enlightenment. As I write about them smiling and weeping here, somewhere far away there will also be smiling and weeping, trembling and dancing.

1
The Women

Matchmaking

Growing up without once having eaten rice would be strange; reaching maturity without some form of romantic encounter would be just as odd.

I was promoted to the rank of cadre in late 1982, with much fanfare. In the spring of 1983, aged twenty-five, I returned home in a blaze of glory, ready to meet a mate. This promotion meant I was no longer a foot soldier and would never have to come back to this village to weather the same storms as my elders. I felt like a bad son. As if I was being disloyal to this soil I'd sprung from. This made me reluctant to tell people I was now an officer. I was unwilling to wear my new four-pocket uniform on the village streets. I kept it secret, feeling as if I'd picked destiny's pocket and couldn't flaunt my spoils openly. Back home, in the small courtyard of the tile-roofed house my parents had devoted all their energies to building for me and my siblings, excitement and joy abounded. I made sure during our first meal together to complain about the inconvenience and suffering of army life. After dinner, by the light of a fifteen-watt lamp, everyone talked solemnly about my matchmaking session the next day. My sister was told to clean the house inside and out, while my mother would head out first thing in the morning to buy the ingredients for noodles with ground pork. As soon as the sun had warmed the rear courtyard, my father would be banished there and wouldn't stir an inch, so my date wouldn't be able to tell he was a sick man. If he moved, he'd start coughing, and phlegm would plague him for the rest of the day.

My father cheerfully accepted his assignment and enthusiastically confirmed he'd had this worry too. He'd already planned to hide himself away during Lianke's date, to prevent the girl from finding out about his chronic illness.

This was a battle we had to win. I felt bad making my father stay out of sight for the sake of a potential marriage, but the thought merely passed through my mind before I let it drift away. It was rare to see my father's face flushed with joy, and I didn't really consider telling him not to hide. Time slipped by and soon the sun was rising, dazzling as always. The earth turned at the same steady rate. The trees by our front gate and on the village green were the same as they had been the day before, and the day before that. Each moment succeeding the one before, time conquering itself. Our family, though, would never be the same again. A few months ago, I'd become an officer of the People's Liberation Army. I'd crossed Henan province, all the way from the east side to the west, a full day of trains and buses, just to get back to the village to meet my match. Like a furnace, love warmed the human race, the family, and the individual (me). The loneliness and desolation of youth might be thawed away by this single encounter. With the arrival of spring, trees would burst into flower.

This would truly be one of the better days of my existence.

My sister cleaned the house and compound thoroughly, sweeping under the tables and leaving the floors so spotless that every shadow had a crisp outline, black against white, making all philosophy, ethics, and power structures seem incredibly stark and clear.

My mother had come back with the groceries and got busy in the kitchen. She didn't have enough limbs and had to borrow Fourth Aunt-in-Law's arms and legs too.

My father ducked into the rear courtyard right after breakfast. Sunlight and his radio were his constant companions, like a gift from life itself, the blood running through his veins.

My date arrived sometime after ten, or maybe eleven, but anyway not at noon like she was supposed to. The matchmaker was someone from our village that I ought to have called "Uncle," a cadre from the next town in his gray uniform. The woman worked in the distribution unit of our town's retail center. She'd taken over the job when her father retired, turning her into someone who "ate commodity rations." She "had a position," which meant she had things to accomplish in life. That word, "position," meant she was a personage of the nation, not a farmer who worked in the fields. Her household registration was in town, and her food was provided by the state. We made a fairly equal match. In the journey of life, we'd ended up on the same platform, or at least we were changing trains at the same station. More importantly, this uncle was a lover of literature who'd read many books and had published poems in *Peony*, the local Luoyang literary magazine. The woman he'd picked for me was also literary, and her poems had also appeared in *Peony*.

There we were, a trio of countryside litterateurs.

"You have a lot in common, there'll be plenty to talk about," the uncle had reassured me. As they approached, some local children darted into our home to yell, "They're coming! They're coming!" My mother and sister shooed the kids away. Then they were here, the uncle striding ahead with my date behind him. The womenfolk welcomed her warmly, and she stepped over our threshold without any sign of shyness, chatting away with the uncle about some town business. She came inside, sat down, accepted the pocket egg that my mother quickly fried for her, stirred the sugar at the bottom of the bowl with her chopsticks, and rested one foot on the opposite knee, shaking her legs. This string of actions and her casual attitude reminded me of when sent-down cadres were billeted with our family. Watching her from one side, I felt dumbstruck, uncomprehending. This didn't feel like a matchmaking session—a mystical, tender, yet enormously consequential romantic encounter. She behaved as if she'd come to our home for an inspection or field study, and because her documentation didn't mention matchmaking, because her superiors hadn't instructed her to fall in love, this visit would have nothing to do with romance.

That's how it was. I stood there like a visitor, like a servant, until the uncle realized and uttered the words, "Go on, sit." Then the romance began, as if the curtains had opened and

I was being puppeteered onto the stage; she was pulling the strings. The sun shone golden yellow. My insides felt like clear water. Outside, the paulownia and elm trees were in full bloom, and the fragrance of honeysuckle wafted unconstrained through our courtyard. The chickens and ducks weren't interfering with our date, but nonetheless my mother and sister shooed them away, then decided to go out, leaving the vast courtyard, the yawning day, the house, and the silence in their entirety to the uncle and the woman and me. I could hear footsteps in the street outside, the faint patter of insect-gnawed paulownia blossoms dropping through the air and hitting the ground.

Mother had given the uncle and the young woman each a plate with four pocket eggs, while I got two. Ten eggs, an offering to my romance. I can't remember if the uncle finished his eggs, but I ate both of mine, while my date only had one before pushing the plate away. She didn't like the earthy smell of countryside eggs, she said. As the uncle and I brought the plates to the kitchen, he said, "Look how generous she's being. You're an army officer, you could stand to be a bit more open." When we got back to the living room, the uncle claimed he had something to take care of and left me and her alone at the crossroads of fate.

And so love began.

My heart thumped like a jackhammer on a paving stone, like thunder rumbling across a field.

Her shining gray eyes, that looked dark from the thick lashes, rested with friendly attention on his face, as though she were recognizing him, and then promptly turned away to the passing crowd,

> as though seeking someone. In that brief look Vronsky had time to notice the suppressed eagerness which played over her face, and flitted between the brilliant eyes and the faint smile that curved her red lips. It was as though her nature were so brimming over with something that against her will it showed itself now in the flash of her eyes, and now in her smile. Deliberately she shrouded the light in her eyes, but it shone against her will in the faintly perceptible smile.[1]

So Tolstoy describes Anna Karenina during her first encounter with Vronsky.

> It was inevitable: the scent of bitter almonds always reminded him of the fate of unrequited love.[2]

The opening line of *Love in the Time of Cholera*, the sound of a door opening to a long romance.

That's how everything began.

That's also how everything ended.

The sunlight in the yard was like satin floating in water. With the farm fowl gone, sparrows supplied their affection, hopping from the yard into the room, openly scratching around for food. On the wall was Chairman Mao's portrait, and below him were a photo of my late grandmother and my grandfather's faded ancestral tablet, all of them decades old but fresh as yesterday. The furniture was silent; the sparrows were chatty. The walls and the wallpaper, the shelves made from planks nailed into the wall, laden with grain and other random items, were all imbued with the history of the village, with reality, with the romantic imagination of humanity. The whole time she had one leg crossed over the other. I didn't think that was appropriate for our first meeting.

Into this silence, our conversation unfolded.

"What bold sparrows," she said with feeling.

I smiled. "You've had poems in *Peony*?"

She shot me a look full of pride.

"I've published a few short stories and a one-act play," I said, trying to sound casual. "All in provincial magazines and the Wuhan area army journal."

"So what?" she said loudly, looking at me again, allowing her foot to sway in the air. I felt like her raised leg and shaking foot took up all the space and time, leaving me unable to say more. As if space and time were her private property, nothing to do with me. I fell quiet, but my silence alerted her: She noticed my eyes were fixed on her foot, lowered it to the floor and looked at me with an indescribable expression.

"My family is very poor," I said to her.

She seemed startled. "I know."

"I suppose you haven't heard that my father's ill?"

"I have." She looked at me solemnly, then abruptly changed the subject. "Is your unit going to war?"

"I don't know." I looked away.

Nothing more to say. My mother, my sister, and the matchmaker came back in with food for a courting couple. The first two bowls of noodles with ground pork went to my date and the matchmaker. The third bowl went to my father, still hidden in the rear courtyard. Despite the spring warmth, he had an old comforter over him. The radio at his feet was playing the Henan opera *Chaoyang Village*, and he was finishing my date's leftover eggs. Grinning, he asked, "How's it going?" I shook my head. "Why not?" he said, shocked. I hesitated. "As soon as she got here, she crossed her legs and kept shaking them."

My father thought about that. "So she's confident. She has a government job."

"It's because she looks down on us," I blurted out with certainty.

He thought some more. "We don't have to live together after you're married. Tell her I won't get in your way."

I thought for what felt like a year. "We'll see," I said to my father, but also to the uncertainty, to the plan to let love into my life. A few days later, I went back to my unit. At the time, we weren't generally allowed to take more than a week off, including traveling time. I wrote her a letter as soon as I arrived, and she replied half a month later. I wrote her again, and twenty days later received her second letter. I wrote her a third time and said, "If you think our relationship isn't suitable, we can end things here." There are many things in life you have to stop halfway. She immediately replied, "You were the one who said it won't work out, not me. Thank you for that!"

And so this relationship, which began with such clamor, fizzled out. A quick beginning, a quick ending, like a gust of wind across a field. There are two more things I need to mention: I've never been able to decide whether she was attractive or not. Five foot four or five, skin a little on the dark side, set off nicely by her ink-black hair. She had the feral beauty of a wilderness. The other thing: The old green train that had brought me from where I was serving in Shangqiu all the way to Luoyang took over six hours to get there, and oddly, over six hours to get back too.

It turned out that in life, coming and going take the same amount of time.

Romance was like the paulownia flowers that bloomed in that season, charming as an awkward yet magnificent smile.

More Matchmaking

The Sino-Vietnamese war that broke out in February 1979 is generally known in China as "The War of Defending Our Borders Against Vietnam." Thanks to this fairly reasonable description, young men and women quickly came to hero-worship our troops, which is to say, if a war hero gave a speech in front of the entire nation, young women would swarm him and he'd drown in letters offering romance, as many as hairs on an ox, as fallen grain in the fields. Then the excitement died down and everyone realized: *Oh my God, people die in wartime!* Young ladies' enthusiasm for marrying soldier boys collapsed, and army camps became mere concentration camps for youths.

Our humanism was all too human, it turns out.

The army didn't always give you time off if your parents were ill, but if an older soldier or officer said they wanted to go home for matchmaking, they'd get approved nine times out of ten. I used my matchmaking leave to help my parents with the harvest, though to be fair I did also meet a date while I was home. In the sixth month of the lunar calendar, with the sun roasting us from high above, you could smell the scorched reek of everyone's crisped hair. Grab at your own scalp and you'd have a palmful of hair ash. As noon approached, the wheat field was covered in the vicious haze of the sun. One day, my father and I were working when a jeep pulled up not far from us, and someone came out onto the ridge between our fields, about a hundred meters away, calling my name and waving so urgently it seemed something significant must have happened in my life or his.

My father and I froze.

"Come quick! Hurry up!"

My eyes focused. The shouting man was Uncle Ji, a distant relative, who was now stamping his feet with anxiety. I dropped my thresher and hurried over to him. When I got close, he said, "Get in!" and shoved me into the back of the jeep.

Belching air, the vehicle pulled away.

We left behind my father, the wheat field, the village, the streets. Swaddled in heat, silence, and sweat, I hunkered down in the ancient jeep and tried to guess what twist in my fate this portended. The man in the driver's seat forging this new path for me was the head of our county's Bureau of Commerce. The bureau head's silence made the atmosphere so solemn you'd have thought we were on our way to an execution ground. He didn't say a single word, and I didn't dare ask any questions. We'd gone quite a few kilometers before he turned to say my father had been fretting himself to pieces and gotten word to Uncle Ji that he was concerned I'd be a bachelor for the rest of my days. Now, he said, everything was sorted. A girl who worked in a Luoyang department store was willing to marry me—I only had to say the word. Furthermore, he added mysteriously, the girl had no idea we were coming that day. We would creep into the store and he'd point her out to me. If I liked what I saw, he'd go tell her so we could meet properly and fall in love. Of course, if I said no, that might hurt her feelings.

She had agreed to our marriage without setting eyes on me.

What's more, this girl wasn't from our village or even the county seat; she was from the provincial capital, Luoyang, where I longed to be. My first reaction was to look down. I had on my usual harvest footwear, an old pair of flip-flops that slipped on and off easily. How could I wear these grubby, worn-out things on a date? I squirmed and my feet writhed, feeling intense shame, as if the girl was staring at my feet right then. Meanwhile, Uncle Ji noticed that my hair was littered with wheat tassels and my face was covered in grime. "That's so disrespectful! We'll find some water and get you cleaned up." The jeep kept speeding toward the city. Dozens of kilometers later, as we passed Longmen Hill, he spotted a mechanical pump spraying water across a field and stopped so I could wash the village dirt and exhaustion off my face, hair, and spirit. When I was done, we drove on, carefree and radiant, to the center of the known world: Luoyang city.

Luoyang was sixty-two kilometers from my village. As we entered the city, my pulse quickened. I've often thought since then that our heart rates must be positively correlated with love. When I'm asked what love is, I answer: "Love" is when you can't stop your heart beating faster because of that special someone. The wide roads, the crisscrossing streets, the constant flow of pedestrians, the tall buildings—was this the sight that greeted Julien Sorel the first time he came to

Paris from the countryside? Telegraph poles evenly spaced along the road, young women cycling home after work, elementary school children holding hands to cross the road. A city's civilization beckoning me. There and then I decided: If this department store girl had agreed to marry me sight unseen, what reason could I possibly have to reject her? As long as she wasn't silly, foolish, or deficient in some other way, I would go along with this marriage and these arrangements for my life. We would face the storms of existence, through thick and thin, growing old together to the bitter end. How old was she? A little older or younger was fine. How tall? An inch more or less could hardly matter. How educated? Eh, I hadn't even finished high school myself. And even if she wasn't pretty, how unattractive could she really be? A city's department store inevitably ends up at the center of its prosperity, the heart of its bustle, its public square. Its most elegant face. Full of crowds in all seasons. A truly hideous person would never get to be a salesclerk there. I wasn't going to be picky. I had nothing to worry about. The sixty-two-kilometer journey passed quickly enough, but once we got into the city, the remaining distance seemed to take as long to navigate as if we were traveling from Beijing to Nanjing or even Tokyo. The road felt endless, our destination far away.

Yet it was just a few kilometers.

The jeep pulled up abruptly outside a tall building. Uncle Ji got out, glanced at his watch, and said we'd arrived at exactly the right time, as if this were the moment in autumn when fruit ripened. I stood by the side of the road while he fussed with my clothes and smoothed my tousled hair. He would point out the girl from the entrance, he told me furtively, then he would walk in like a regular customer. This felt like a scene from a gangster movie: Having agreed on our secret code, we strode into the department store. Good thing my heart didn't jump clean out of my chest, like a rabbit congratulating itself on surviving another winter and finally being able to leap without landing in a snowdrift. She was on the first floor, though I can't remember now if she was selling fabric or clothes. Those two items are close enough that it's understandable I would mix them up. This isn't amnesia; I was just so excited and nervous that I didn't notice (or care) what was around her, or even what she was wearing.

When a crimson flower blooms, no one cares if there are leaves around it.

She was so beautiful that I stopped in my tracks while the city flowed around me. I'd looked where Uncle Ji's finger was pointing and knew right away who he meant. Neither tall nor short, skin a little tan (like the previous one—I guess that was my fate), face like a ripe fruit, eyes darting around as she added up a customer's purchases. I felt as if I'd seen her somewhere before. This instant familiarity made me believe in the mystical nature of marriage. I decided I would fall in love with her. We would get married and have kids. I would suffer the worst of times with her, all the way to the end.

Uncle Ji pointed at her for all of one second, and it took me less than a second to decide I would marry her. "See her?" he whispered. I nodded with unusual certainty. "The one in sky blue, not dark gray." His insistence felt as unnecessary as weeds by the side of the road. He leaned over again to murmur that marriage was the most important event in a person's life, even more crucial than something like becoming emperor. I needed to be absolutely sure I'd thought this through. Yes meant yes, no meant no, and I couldn't just go along with this because she'd said yes first.

With that, Uncle Ji melted into the crowd, leaving me lost in thought by the entrance. As he disappeared, I turned my attention and focus onto the woman, her appearance, her clothes, her bustling movements. Yes, I was willing to live with her, and I was certain that marrying her was an unimpeachable choice. Then I noticed she was looking my way, and in a panic I retreated back outside.

The sky was intensely blue, as open and clear as my heart. Life and the world were so beautiful. I felt a jolt of gratitude toward my parents for bringing me into existence.

After a bean-sized segment of time, Uncle Ji emerged from the store, his face aglow. Standing on Zhongzhou Middle Road in the heart of Luoyang, with the earth and sky and trees as our witnesses, I knew this was the most consequential, solemn moment of my whole life and my entire family's fate.

"So?" he asked.

With great confidence, I nodded.

He smiled. "I need you to say yes or no."

I beamed too. "Yes."

"Wonderful. I'll let her parents know, and while I'm there we'll fix a day too."

And so, almost by chance and without careful consideration, the curtain rose on yet another romance, just as certain as daylight coming with the sunrise, as flowers appearing even in the dankest hilltop nooks in springtime. Uncle Ji and his jeep pulled away. He'd told me to wait by the department store entrance, that he'd be back very soon having "fixed a day." We'd arrived at one in the afternoon and spent about eight minutes inside, but it took him a whole three hours to return. During that time, hunger came over me like a storm. I longed to grab some food from the restaurant across the road, but I didn't have a cent on me. I sat on the curb like an abandoned child, looking up at the sky, watching the passersby. When Uncle Ji got back, I thought, the first thing I'd do is get a bowl of noodles. At a little past four, the jeep sputtered to a halt in front of me. Uncle Ji got out. His face was green, as if he'd just been punched. He stared at the department store, at the noodle stalls next to him, at the flow of people. After a moment's hesitation, he said, "Let's go. We can talk more at home."

We got in.

We went home.

More than two hours later, the jeep stopped by the wheat field. The last glimmers of sunset blazed like fire. Uncle Ji was a man of few words, but he managed to say on the way home, "Let's never mention this again." After dropping me off, he waved at my father, who was still harvesting, and said he was so terribly busy, with endless meetings each day that left him sweating, so he wouldn't stop by our home. Instead, he gave me a message to pass on to my father: He didn't need to worry about me finding a mate. Now that I was a cadre and an army officer, surely someone would come along.

In 1989 or 1990, by which time I was not only married but had a child of four or five, I was studying literature at the People's Liberation Army Academy of Art in Beijing.

We visited home that New Year, and on the second day, which is traditionally when you see your relatives, Uncle Ji—long retired by then—came to our home with a gift basket. Smiling, he told me the Luoyang department store girl had seen an article about me in the *Luoyang Daily*—a color photo of me beneath the headline "Luoyang District Produces a Talent"—and she'd gone round to his place to complain that he never mentioned, back when he'd first introduced me, that I was a literature lover who wrote fiction. "She and her whole family regret turning you down. Well, let them regret it!" he chortled. Only then did I find out that the young woman's mother was Uncle Ji's wife's sister. The reason I'd found her familiar at first sight is that she looked a lot like Uncle Ji's eldest daughter.

After processing this new information, I smiled awkwardly at him.

All too often, an awkward smile after something ends carries its own kind of beauty.

Interlude 1

There's a meandering sort of talk you could call an interlude.

Let memory stand on tiptoe and creep up behind me as I recollect my experiences of seeking a mate. The word "fate" stands like a boundary marker on the road of my life. But then one day, you return to that junction, grope for the marker, and realize this so-called destiny is mere coincidence. Buddha calls these chances, random encounters, and partings "destiny," obscuring the incomprehensibility of randomness and covering it up.

In fact, all fate is decided by chance.

It's only when chance meets chance that something becomes inevitable.

If my first date hadn't sat in such a swaggering way, what would our fate have been? Such a tiny, short-lived moment with such profound, far-reaching consequences. Terrifying if you think too much about it. Like a train driver having to jam on the brakes because an ant is crossing the tracks.

If Uncle Ji had been more eloquent and talked the Luoyang department store girl into accepting me, would I now have a family with her?

In our lives, our movements, our labors, we are not searching for certainty in the midst of randomness, but rather for chance encounters within the predetermined. When you accept that happenstance guides your life, that it is the key to your fate, you can let go of many things, free yourself, and face your destiny head-on. Even if you were to step through the wrong door and end up in jail, you'd simply say to yourself, chastened—

Well, that's life!

First Encounter

1

Turns out our fates are determined by chance.

Turns out we struggle through life to encounter the random chances allotted to us.

I have no idea when or what the chance was that abruptly moved my life from the countryside to the city, abandoning a farmer's life for an urban one. Maybe it was when my father raised his pickax high in the air, or when my mother took stock of her life and heaved a long sigh. Or maybe it was on the way home from school, when I spotted the commune's cadres holding their water flasks, humming and tapping their spoons on their plates as they stood in line at the cafeteria. Somehow, as soon as I had any awareness of the world, I decided that I would flee the countryside before I died, that I would make my way to a city.

Live or die, I would become a city person!

I hadn't skipped any of the steps in the young rural person's creed—"Show your cunning, stand out from the crowd, marry, and enter the city"—nor was I outstanding in any way. When I was in the army, I went to bed one night with the company's brooms and shovels beneath my covers so I could wake up before reveille the next day and do the cleaning by myself, reaping all the glory and praise. When I wanted to join the Party, I left a twelve-yuan satin coverlet from the county silk factory under the pillow of each commander and instructor, even though my stipend was only six yuan a month. When we planted crops at the weekend, I went along with the other soldiers, rolling up our trouser legs, jumping into the toilet pit and using both hands to break off frozen chunks of shit and piss. On top of that, a month before July 1 (the founding of the Chinese Communist Party) and August 1 (the founding of the People's Liberation Army), I'd write odes and encomiums celebrating the Party and army and send them to the papers to be published in time for those occasions.

I scrubbed my sergeant's feet. I washed my deputy commander's socks and underwear.

Once, after being unable to vault the pommel horse or swing over the high bar during training, I got up at two in the morning and practiced alone till dawn.

At the marksmanship competition for new recruits, I was somehow able to score a hundred points with ten shots. The next day, representing the entire regiment at the division tournament, I crouched down a hundred meters from the target and scored ninety-eight points with ten shots. Our regiment commander was so thrilled he kept smacking my head, as if he'd found an Easter egg without even looking for it. An endless stream of praise and awards, prizes and achievement—the door of fate opened before me and light poured through, humanity's radiance illuminating the path of my future. I joined the army in October 1978. Three months later, war broke out on the Vietnamese border, and the troops plunged into fear, excitement, and anxiety. Everyone fervently wrote letters begging for the chance to fight, while quietly praying the conflict would end before we could be sent to the front. I'm sure this terror behind a façade of courage could be found in every camp. I lived this reality too, stricken with dread even as I copied other people's letters and sent them to our commanders. Yet I rolled my eyes with jaded skepticism at those who bit their fingertips so they could write their letters in blood. I spent almost three years amid this consternation and unease, yearning for promotion but also fearing a higher rank meant staying in the army longer, which increased my chances of getting hauled to the front line. In 1981, a large group of soldiers who'd achieved glory at the front returned to the camp in all their magnificence, many now promoted, swelling our numbers from four to five or six platoons. Each platoon leader or instructor's chair now had to accommodate two asses. Same for the regiments. And so, taking the long view, the higher-ups issued an unexpected proclamation: Soldiers would no longer be plucked directly from the ranks for promotion but needed to have been through the military academy or army educational institute (roughly equivalent to trade school) and also to be a Party member, squad leader, or deputy squad leader aged twenty or younger. If you fell short of any of these requirements, you weren't eligible.

I was a squad leader and Party member, but I'd already been past the cutoff age when I joined up. The disappointment slackened something in me—the unraveling of despair.

Promotion was out of my reach. No point yearning for it.

In a world without wolves, sheep may wander carefree.

I requested a discharge and began thinking about my future. I was a Party member, and the village branch secretary was pushing me to go back and take the role of headman. Effectively, I'd be a branch secretary on our village committee. On the other hand, several of my stories had made it from my handwritten drafts into print, and if fortune were to shine on me, it was not impossible that I could go to the county cultural institute or library and become "someone with a position." I decided to go home. The higher-ups said I was talented and tried persuading me to stay, but I was a rabbit who simply had to make the transition from my springtime warren to my autumn shelter, my winter burrow.

The winter of 1981 was like any other winter. Clouds roiled above the vast plains of East Henan and leaves fell endlessly. The silence of humanity trod the main streets of Shangqiu city, saying a sad farewell with its footsteps. "Goodbye! Goodbye!" In my pocket was a 120-yuan discharge bonus and sixty-five kilograms of national ration coupons, two months' worth. I'd bought my parents each a new set of clothes and other gifts, along with more presents for my brother, his wife, and my sisters, plus pastries and snacks, and cigarettes and lighters: the obligatory offerings for everyone I would meet back home. The old green train for discharged troops was at Shangqiu station, as it had been when I arrived, as if it hadn't moved in the three years since it first brought me to this camp on the plains, as if it had been waiting for me and the other village youths to return home.

There was a riot of firecrackers, drums, and cymbals on this run-down train platform. When people are at their lowest, they light bonfires in the wilderness to soothe their spirits. Virtually all the discharged men were sobbing. Their comrades, here to say goodbye, smiled and waved as they brushed away their tears. For some reason, I felt neither sadness nor joy nor any other emotion. I didn't wave goodbye and saw no point in hugging anyone. I overheard two friends bidding each other farewell. One said, tearfully, "If they don't promote you or let you into the Party next year, you ought to leave too." The other's reply made my very soul tremble: "I'm waiting to go to war. If I set foot on the front line, I'll die happy."

At the carriage door, another pair of buddies shared a delightful exchange. One said, "Write me, and don't tell my girlfriend I didn't even make squad leader." The other one turned back to wave from the steps of the carriage. "When

I marry her, I'll send you cigarettes and wedding candy—" Cheerful cries warmed the platform and the sky above. How good-hearted people are. Also, noisy. The world seemed full of humankind's love, sorrow, passion, as well as its cat-and-mouse scheming. Hefting my luggage through the crowd, I clambered into a rear carriage. Dazed blankness, as if the entire sky and vast East Henan plains had been emptied out. For some reason, the thought came to me that I'd joined the army to escape the countryside and come to the city, and I'd wanted to get married and have children here, so I wouldn't be bound to the soil like my parents, enduring all seasons and weathers outside. And yet, after three years of struggle, currying favor and anxiety, I was returning to my village after all. Back to the land. As a pig must return to its sty, a dog its kennel. As oxen and horses are harnessed again to their reins and made to till the earth.

Tears came to my eyes.

My sorrow at my fate mingled with everyone else's. Winter sun warmed the air. Commotion on top of commotion. Was time speeding up or slowing down? Why couldn't we leave right away? A sudden departure, a final farewell. But the train remained stubbornly still. Trying to get away from the agitation and sadness, I tossed my rucksack and other stuff in a corner and sat atop the pile staring into space, letting the goodbyes clump together so I could kick them away, snapping the long threads that bound people.

I sat numbly in a corner of the carriage.

People looked askance. Comrades came over to comfort me: "You've made it into the Party—wasn't it all worth it? Why the long face?"

Our military armbands and beret insignias didn't have a single scrap of bright red. How hideous they looked, I thought. Like an exquisite youth minus his sparkling eyes. There were those who, like me, had taken off their uniforms and bought outfits in blue, black, or dark gray, but not one of these new looks suited them.

I observed the chaos in the carriage and heard the firecrackers and percussion outside, and the stirring, tragic music blaring from the propaganda truck's speakers.

Our departure time drew close. Over the speakers came an announcement for the soldiers who weren't traveling to please leave the train. I was leaving this waystation of my life, this smoky fire tower, for somewhere more desolate or peaceful. Through the window, all I could see were waving hands and wide-open mouths shouting something. Footsteps rampaging with no order at all, like on market day. Then in an instant, the chaos stilled, a path opened through the crowd, and my commanding officer's brand-new jeep zoomed down the platform. It overshot and had to brake abruptly. My commander stumbled out and ran back toward us, yelling.

The train windows were open and crammed with gawking eyes. Some of those heads turned back into the carriage, to look at me. Before anyone could work out what was going on, we heard the commander climb the stairs and bellow, "Where is Yan Lianke?"

I scrambled to my feet. Like a missile, the strapping form of the commander blasted directly at me. He smacked me on the head and said, urgently, "You're getting promoted. Grab your stuff and come with me!"

I stood there blankly, as if I hadn't heard him.

A dazzling smile spread across his face. The Wuhan District Performing Arts Troupe had collectively taken first prize at the national finals in Beijing, he said, and to reward our talent, the director general of the General Political Department had approved some names for promotion, so these superb actors, singers, and musicians could remain in their unit. I was on the list because the audience and director general loved my one-act play *Hanging Two Banners*, for which I'd won something called the Program Prize. The commander got the phone call and came rushing to stop the train so he could bring me, my luggage, and my discharge papers back to camp.

This was the most unexpected, unasked-for summons of my life. It wasn't just me getting struck by the beloved hammer of destiny; every soldier around me looked dazed, as if flatbreads had fallen from the sky and whacked them silly. The entire carriage fell silent. All eyes were on the commander's face and on my fate. At that moment, a thought flashed through my mind: *My God, is the war still going on?*

When I said nothing, the commander glanced at his watch and said, "How about this? If you accept the promotion, get off the train. Otherwise, stay on and go home."

"May I talk it over with my parents?" This felt like the most appropriate, respectful thing I could say.

He thought about it. "I'll give you a week. Be back within seven days and the promotion is yours. If not, I'll send your paperwork back upstairs."

And that's how it was.

Let there be light, and there was light.

Let there be water, and there was water.

When your life gets a boost from destiny and the old green train suddenly turns into an express, these twists and turns in the track, forging ahead or turning back, seem disconnected from anyone else. I'd almost been flung from the carriage of fate, but a few seconds before my departure, the powers above suddenly remembered literature and the arts and chose to give humankind something for our souls. It's not enough for them to ensure our survival; we need spiritual nourishment too.

Who cares if these objects are only sometimes souls, and at other times merely clumps of flesh around a soul?

Thanks be to destiny!

Thanks be to these appendages of our flesh—literature and creativity!

2

That's how it happened.

Let there be light, and there was light.

The idea of me going straight back into the army with a promotion right after my discharge didn't leave my family surprised or overjoyed, but rather led to a night of unease and silence. At the time, gunshots from the Vietnamese border echoed constantly through every corner of China. My unit hadn't yet been deployed to the front, but soldiers are food for the hunger of war, and everyone felt the same anguish. When I got home that evening and told my family that my unit wanted me back, the prospect didn't delight them. It wasn't just the war; my father's health had been deteriorating. My brother had moved away for his new job, and both my sisters were married. My family needed me to work in the fields and care for my parents. Instead, I got home and immediately told my parents about the promotion. I'd asked my commander to bring my rucksack back to camp, I said, since I'd be returning soon.

This "rucksack" was actually just the blanket that had moldered for three years on my bunk, rolled into a bundle; I could easily have done without it, but leaving it in the camp showed that I intended to be back. No one said a word after dinner, confused and uncertain as they were about whether I ought to go back and accept this promotion. This dragged on late into the night, until my brother finished his shift and cycled fifteen kilometers home along the canal in the dark. He hurried in and told my parents that Lianke enjoyed writing, which would do him no good if he came home. It was the arts that needed a person like Lianke, so could we pull any strings to get him there?

"Let him go. I can deal with anything that comes up." My brother's words cut through the family's tangled thoughts, and they agreed I ought to escape the land and return to the army. We still needed someone to plant crops and take care of my parents, and the answer was obvious: Find Lianke a wife. She'd take care of things at home, leaving him free to return to his unit and accept promotion.

The best of both worlds. Yet the great wish of my life was to leave the countryside and set up home in the city!

Here was our way out. I was twenty-three, after all, and it was high time to find a mate. Back then, if you were still unmarried at twenty-two, people said you were left on the shelf. Even so, I was surprised that my courtship became just another item in the order of business, with such speed you'd have thought the order came directly from Central Command. Marriage was first mentioned on the morning of my second day home, and that very afternoon, the doctor showed up at our home with young women from our village.

Sunlight. A small courtyard. The uneasy joy of an entire family. My hapless cowardice and silence. I'd never, not in my whole life, thought about what kind of person I wanted to marry. I'd never considered how love would begin, how it might unfold. Not even what love was made of or what it weighed, what proportion of its significance was emotional or physical, or which was more important: spiritual or sensual love. Now I think that's like asking whether planting or harvesting matters more. I had no sense of direction, no sense of color, no sense of language—and no sense of eros. In *Blindness*, we are told of the blind women that "what terrified them was not so much the rape" but rather, as one of them thinks to herself, "the worst thing of all is that I might feel some pleasure."[3] Saramago truly understood humanity. He knew that one person is as incomprehensible to another as the heavens themselves.

The little courtyard, the sunlight, the chill and warmth of winter that year. Just like that, the day was here. For generations, the role of the matchmaker in Chinese weddings had been an easily mocked amalgamation of chicanery, flattery, and lies. Yet over thousands of years of unflagging marital history, with the implacable growth of our population, matchmakers have played an essential role.

Around three or four in the afternoon, two young women came into our home with the matchmaker. The taller one was slender, the shorter one a little plump. Their faces were bright red as they took their seats. After a short while, the matchmaker ushered me into a side room, then summoned the tall, thin one. "Talk, talk." He left and shut the door. The tiny window didn't let in much light, so we turned on the lamp even though it was midafternoon. This south-facing room on the east side of the house had been my bedroom before I joined the army. Bed, desk, walls plastered with old newspapers, ceiling of crisscrossed reeds with more newspapers forming a canopy between them—everything felt thoroughly familiar, as if I'd never left. I'd first started writing in this room. She took a seat in the very chair I sat in to write my first story, when not a soul knew what I was doing. I sat on the edge of the bed, a few feet away. We stared at each other in silence, then we both looked down. I'd never before felt the sheer weight of time. Every second pressed down on our skulls and dignity, like we were bugs living beneath a stone tablet. It was very still. Time bowed down our heads and shoulders, and the rest of our lives. Was she waiting for me to speak first? Was I supposed to ask something like, "Are you up for it?" But I didn't. I feared she would blurt out the question. Luckily, she didn't either. The oppressive silence only lasted a few minutes, until she abruptly looked up at me and scurried from the room.

To the kitchen to help my mother with dinner.

In between rinsing the vegetables and cooking the food, she grabbed a broom and swept up every scrap of trash and coal ash from the kitchen and courtyard, brought it outside and tossed it onto next door's rubbish heap. When I saw her helping my mother with the housework, my heart sank to unseen depths. She was already behaving like my parents' daughter. She picked up my father's spittoon, emptied out his asthmatic phlegm and cleaned it out, just the way my sisters did. This marriage was unavoidable. There was no retreat.

Kind and hardworking. Doing all this without a word.

I left the room and stood in the courtyard for a while, then went to the backyard and stared into space. The backyard was divided in two, with a paulownia tree and two elms. When war broke out in February 1979, my father paced here all day and night, sunk in thought. He couldn't understand why people had to fight, why they couldn't live in peace. The trees witnessed how much my father missed his son, how much he worried, until his body gave in. My father handed his unfinished life to me. Now it was my turn to be lost in thought here. All of this—war or the mere act of survival, marriage or love, kindness and beauty—was part of the entanglement of life and fate. My father took everything he wasn't able to figure out and handed it to me. The paulownia and elm trees that had borne witness to my father's pondering now observed my wordless silence, until the matchmaker-doctor popped into the backyard. "Not bad, right? Nice-looking and a hard worker. Just the sort of person your family needs." With a broad grin, he went back inside. I don't know what kind of jubilant negotiations took place after that, but my second sister came running out and said to me, sounding very serious, "You agreed to marry her?"

I gaped at her.

"If you don't want to marry her, you need to tell them right now, or it'll be too late."

That was the most righteous thing she ever said to me,

both as a sister and as a woman. Yet somehow I wasn't able to say, "I don't agree," just as to this day I've never been able to say, "I love you!" with any seriousness. This cowardice is chronic and is as much a part of my life as my eyes and nose. Being bad at saying no has turned me into what I am today, a person shaped by the wind and the soil. The northern trees and plants, hills and rivers, sky and weather, are what make northerners northerners.

That's how I acquired a fiancée.

I remember the engagement present my mother gave her family: a hundred yuan. They tried over and over to refuse this tiny sum of money. My father wasn't well, they said, we should use it to pay for his medications. I often think about how kindness might be a virtue, but in a woman it can easily lead to tragedy. A man's kindness slides and falls into the abyss of his uselessness. In a woman, in womankind, it often leads to a life of desolation. I'm not saying evil leads to all that is good in life; I'm just asking what kind of soil produces bitterness in apples, what makes the sweet apricots and pears that grow on trees remain apricots and peaches, yet once plucked and in the world, they turn into dried apricots, dried pears, or rotten fruit? Why is it that in this world, men's kindness is often hapless, while women's kindness brings about evil or tragedy?

3

I went back to the army but didn't become a cadre right away.

This kind of promotion is a major event. A commander from God-knows-where decided that all of us in the Wuhan

District Cultural Troupe had to go through half a year of specialist training before we could be allowed into the officer ranks. The musicians and singers were sent to the Central Command Cultural Troupe, while I and the other literary types ended up in the editorial department of *Battle Arts*, one of the magazines run by the Cultural Troupe. This "study and training" was actually answering phones and fetching mail, returning used newspapers to their binders, opening unsolicited submissions with scissors and reading them in search of "eye-catching" essays, stories, or poems.

A long period of waiting and anxiety. Other people were worried they'd fail to qualify and get discharged. I had an additional concern: If I *did* get promoted, how would I live with my mate? We'd only met twice, including the matchmaking session. A few days later, just before I left for camp, she came round again to say goodbye. No tokens of love or keepsakes, just a sack of grain her family had been keeping in reserve.

I said goodbye and departed.

I wrote her a letter when I got to camp, and she soon replied. That's when all my problems started. The scorching hot Wuhan summer delighted the mosquitoes, who sang all day long. One October evening, the Cultural Troupe commander who'd pushed for all of us to become cadres showed up at my accommodation block with his daughter and a basket of bananas. He said a few things about the training and our progress and mentioned the stories I was writing. Eventually, he shamefacedly handed over an open envelope and said he was very sorry, this got sent to the editorial department and they naturally assumed it was an unsolicited submission, so they opened it. They stopped reading as soon as they realized it was from my fiancée. He hoped I didn't mind, but a photo fell out of the envelope; everyone thought she was a nice-looking woman and offered their congratulations. We lapsed into silence. The electric fan rattled away. Beads of sweat clustered ponderously on my face. The little girl clamored to go home so he scooped her up. Just before going, he urged me to try a banana—this year's Hubei crop was particularly good, with a subtle sweetness never before seen in history or the present. As he turned to leave, he suddenly stopped and asked delicately, "Your fiancée—what's her level of education?"

I mopped the sweat off my face. "Elementary school."

"Oh." Still carrying his daughter, he walked out, but he only got a few steps before turning back to say, very solemnly, "Out of everyone in this batch, you're the one who might become a real author. I also came to the city from a farming village, but I didn't get married till I'd been promoted—and my wife comes from Wuhan." He looked me in the eye, searching for something in my expression. "There's nothing wrong with having a wife from the countryside. What I mean is ..." He paused to move his daughter to the crook of his other arm. "What I mean is ... For your own sake, if you want to break things off with your fiancée, first make sure she won't denounce you to the Party or show up here and cause a scene."

Having said his piece, he left.

Another mission complete. His footsteps were light and quick, and his shadow stretched from that era all the way into my memory. This is making me recall the marriage and subsequent fate of someone from my unit who worked in the news department. After his promotion, he got engaged to a woman in the city and broke things off with his fiancée back home. A few days after his marriage, the village girl sent a letter to Central Command denouncing him. As punishment for his fickleness, they gave him an official warning and a major demerit and ordered him to settle things with his former fiancée. If she complained again, he would lose his Party membership and new rank. In all this kerfuffle, the worst thing wasn't the former fiancée's grievance. When his new city wife heard he'd had another woman back home, she smashed their cooking pots, flung crockery at him, and smacked him hard across the face. From then on, he was under her thumb. Apart from his work of reading and writing, he had to do all the cooking and laundry, and whenever she was in a bad mood, she would rail at him till she'd vented all her anger.

Then there was a man in our village a bit older than me who did his bit a few years before me to "protect our homes and nation." After much struggle and humiliation, he clawed his way to promotion, but a few days before the final stamp on his paperwork, his fiancée came to visit. He got her a room at the visitors' center, and they were canoodling there after dinner when there was a blackout. Just like that, the brightly lit world plunged into primeval darkness. The visitors' center, the camp, the whole world was nothing but black. Only by lighting a candle could you illuminate the human heart. But they chose not to light a candle, nor did they emerge from the darkened room.

Half an hour of love in the dark.

Thirty minutes later, the electricity was fixed. Light, order, discipline and human consciousness returned to the camp, to the world, just as it had been before. The next day, the higher-ups brought my fellow villager in for a chat and informed him he was no longer in line for promotion. During the blackout the night before, he and his fiancée hadn't come out of the room, nor had they lit any of the candles they'd been provided with. In this cave-like gloom, like the dawn of man, what could he and she have gotten up to in the dark while everyone else stood in the light?

What could they possibly have been doing?

And *then* what did they do?

No amount of explanation did any good, nor could he prove his innocence.

That was back when romance was shameful, a vast, airtight era when every part of the country's apparatus overlapped and connected with every element of human nature. Each of these elements—thought, emotion, nerves, soul, and so on—was a component of that machinery. No one could possibly have broken free of these definitions of love and marriage, nor of this era's bizarre vengeances, grudges, honors, disgraces, or urges. Virtue was built upon the will of the country and the significance of the times, and so was beauty. We weren't just boxed in by factories, mines, school, shops, and streets but also in our thoughts and feelings, in marriage and lovemaking.

My fellow villager's name was struck from the promotion list as easily as picking a blade of grass.

Just like that, he was discharged and sent back home.

His fiancée was now the guilty, evil person who'd destroyed

his entire future. After they were married, she bore his children and waited on him hand and foot, but there was no way she could ever make up for the damage she'd caused him and his entire family. If she hadn't loved him so, if during that half hour of darkness she hadn't adoringly wrapped her arms around him and rested her head on his shoulder, he and she and their children could all have been city dwellers.

Fate really can turn on a dime. After saying goodbye to the commander, I went back into my room, and in the dim yellow light, I thought of how times had changed. I no longer lived in the same era as that other villager, when the visitors' center was surrounded by high walls and metal fencing. The early eighties contained so many of China's turning points, but the light was still light, people were still people, and I remained myself. I stood there for a while, then I took my fiancée's letter from the envelope my commander handed me. A white envelope, standard in this era, with scissor marks where it had been cut open. She'd written her letter on paper marked with a red grid. Before I could finish the half page, I felt like my eyes were being pierced—not by her words, but from the words she didn't know how to write, which she'd replaced with romanized pinyin. About a quarter of the characters were rendered in this way, which made the letter look like it was in code. We'd exchanged letters before, and her eccentric writing style hadn't bothered me then—I knew she'd only been through two years of elementary school, and writing pinyin simply showed how hard she was trying. Things felt different now. This private matter was known to others. A scab had ripped off and bloody pus was gushing from the wound. As others pointed and laughed, the gore puddled into something that looked like a flower but definitely wasn't one. Her photo fell from the envelope. A one-inch headshot that could only have come from a studio, colorized by hand. Her face was as innocent, kind, determined, and unadorned as ever. And yet, in that instant, my world was flooded with shame from all directions, streams of shame pouring onto me from one source: her. In that long moment, people no longer seemed like people. I was no longer me. Evil rose in my heart. Demons took over my soul. I would no longer think of her. I would no longer care about the era, the Party, my parents, or my village. I was no longer me. I was the true me. I was my era, my life, my fate. At the same time, I was none of these things.

In the midst of these muddled thoughts, I decided to burn my bridges. I would move in the direction of destroying other people and trusting myself.

To prevent her next letter from landing in the editorial department's mail sack to get cut open with scissors once again, I endured another half month of training in Wuhan before I could return to Shangqiu Camp. Only then did I write her another letter, long and substantial as the Great Wall, breaking our engagement. Thinking back, I must have written several thousand sorrys and used all the talent of a literary lover, all the hypocrisy and falsehood of a man, to endlessly express my "helplessness" and how "it has to be this way." So many excuses, so many pretty regrets. Presumably that's why, in her long reply days later, she enumerated everything she'd done for my family, as well as all the ways I'd been as evil and disloyal as the heartless opera villain Chen Shimei. Her parting shot was, "Don't worry, I'm not going to come to your unit and denounce you. I won't write a letter either. I know you'd be finished if I did that. You'd lose your promotion and be forced to come back to work on the land like me. I don't blame you, Yan Lianke. I blame my poor education and my bad fate. I blame us all for being peasants and only wanting better lives."

There were no mistakes or blanks in this letter, not a single use of pinyin. To this day, I have no idea who she asked to write this on her behalf. The handwriting was good, as upright and impeccable as her conduct. I still have this letter. If she or someone else were someday to find the letter I sent her, would this world and my family smile at me, or would they fly into a rage?

4

From an early age, my life was like a novel.

When reality presents a story whose sheer force triumphs over any fiction, I can only blush for the limits of the novelist's imagination. This shame impels me, a fiction writer, to kneel before life itself, just as a repentant apostate will prostrate himself before his god.

A little before my son turned two, my wife and I brought him back to my hometown for the first time, to celebrate the New Year. Tianhu was the same as ever, the main street still ran east to west, the sky above the train station looked as it always had, and the village's weeds, scrap paper, and winter fog accompanied the north wind, chattering as they strolled across the desolate waste. I'd finally turned the page on the question of marriage. We had a child who filled in almost all the gaps and deficiencies in my life. The three of us walked hand in hand, like every happy family in the world, laden with luggage and satchels and all kinds of objects, presenting everyone we ran into with cigarettes, chatting with warmth and the hometown accent I'd made sure to rediscover, everything we ought to have, all complete, as perfectly formed as the full moon that would rise above the village on the fifteenth day of the year. But then, as we approached the crossroad on the main street, I spotted someone walking toward me.

That's right, it was *her*!

In a few short years, I'd struggled through many defeats on the matchmaking front, finally fled from the countryside, and attained the dream I'd clung to all through my adolescence and youth: a marriage in the city, a perch where I could rest my ugly, weary feet. Now she who had relinquished me seemed intent on seeing me again. A little girl of three or four tugged at her left sleeve, another girl of two or three tugged at her right, and a third daughter was clutched to her bosom. As we approached, I realized she was pregnant, her belly bulging like the blue cloth bundle on her back. She moved slowly, shuffling her feet, bearing the entire burden of the dark fate I'd condemned her to, as if the bitter sorrow of every village woman in the world was weighing down on her.

I froze there in the street. Glancing frantically around, I spotted a men's toilet placed there by God himself. In a frenzy, I hurried in with my son. When I think back to the awkwardness and embarrassment of that moment, I know that grimy toilet is exactly where I belonged, but I shouldn't have dragged my son in there with me.

After doing various unnecessary things, I figured I'd wasted enough time and came back out. Hand in hand with my wife and son, we headed home as if nothing had happened. In the days that followed, during our New Year's visits, someone I knew very well told me that soon after I got promoted, she'd married into a clan deep in the mountains, dozens of miles from our town. Her husband had a position—he was a miner in a state-owned coal company. After having three daughters in a row, she'd decided to have a fourth child—more than was allowed under the new family planning regime—and had come back home to avoid detection. Then fate had brought us face to face.

It was also fate that tore us apart again, and cast me into a pit of human excrement.

Interlude 2

It's hard to imagine, but for a very long time, our people failed to turn marriage into the business of the individual and the family, allowing it to remain an institution that the era forced you into. Even after we stepped over the threshold of 1949 and accepted the idea of "revolutionary marriage," leaving behind the arranged matches and social hierarchies of before, there were still decades when love and marriage, family, freedom, and privacy were under great strain. For far too long, the marriages of too many people who were considered "public servants" or "key personnel" came under the remit of the times they lived in. Who you loved and were loved by required the investigation, permission, and official seal of the Party. Ditto who you didn't love and weren't loved by. God truly was dead, but the stamp of approval nonetheless existed like one of his fingers. Our entire lives were controlled by those seals, and very few documents could get away from that dread mark.

In my short-lived yet all-too-long matchmaking journey, like everyone else, I had my pick of others and was picked at in return. A relative's big sister in Luoyang once introduced me to another young woman who worked at a ping-pong ball factory there. The sister wrote to ask for a photo, my height, body measurements, and weight. I stared at her letter for a long time before responding, "Why? Am I being sized up like a pig in the market?" I'd forgotten that in the eighties, with the winds of change blowing from the West and Hong Kong, the search for a mate got wrapped up in so-called "vital statistics." In 1983, a villager who'd joined the army a few years before me had gotten married. He worried for me, a twenty-five-year-old bachelor, and decided I should get to know a lady of his acquaintance. Her father was the head of our county's Armed Forces Department, and she was training to be an army nurse in our unit. I felt sure she was out of my league. Filled with trepidation, I decided to knock on the door of matrimony anyway. I boldly wrote her a letter, and she responded with polite restraint. Not receiving a frigid rejection made me think spring was arriving, and with my comrade's heated encouragement, I wrote her a more fervent, lyrical letter. Her response was once again lukewarm, which we decided meant it was time to go scorched-earth.

I understood that in any battle, the aggressor takes the initiative and has all the power. I summoned my literary talent and vast vocabulary and unleashed this magnificent bombast and mellifluous phraseology on her. I wonder if she still has this letter. I imagine it's one of the most nauseating proposals in all of history. A week went by, and she hadn't replied. Two weeks. A month. My comrade and I fretted like farmers who'd planted wheat and couldn't wait for the harvest. Around that time, I happened to have a short story published in a new magazine, *Tokyo Literature*, and my God, it was the featured piece! My comrade rushed to buy a copy at the post office to send to his acquaintance, who replied shortly, "If he's so great, he should apply to university. He doesn't have any qualifications, does he?"

I'd forgotten this was the time of qualifications. Trade school, junior college, and university were the gold pieces that bought you marriage, a passport to promotion. When I look back at my frenzied rush into this proposal, I can see that marriage has always been a part of the times we live in. It was never merely between an individual and his family. Or rather, our couplings and our destinies are manipulated by the times at every moment, including right now, when marriage and sex are relatively individualized.

As it turns out, after smashing the convention of arranged marriages that had endured for thousands of years, the institution of marriage quietly slipped under the heading of revolution, but true reform didn't take place, and we never regained individual control of marriage. Only a lucky few, or those who knew how to get around the times, were able to enter marriages that weren't artefacts of their era. Finding a marriage that wasn't entangled with gaining an advantageous match for your family took enormous courage, intellect, sacrifice, and good fortune. The official stamp was the most visible symbol of the era and its power over the institution of marriage. We needed to work hard to loosen its stranglehold on us. Now, over forty years after so-called reform and opening up, when the country seems to be prosperous enough that we could redefine what it means to be poor and to survive, I think about how love, marriage, and divorce no longer come with so many official stamps and thumbprints. That's the most valuable legacy that history has left to all of us, individuals and families.

Escape and Predestination

In any marriage, you enter through a wide door, then walk toward a second, narrower door.

Who in the world hasn't benefitted from marriage? Yet who hasn't been harmed by it?

In any case, my marriage was a matter of escape and predestination. Quarreling, compromise, bringing each other comfort, growing old together—all for the sake of escape and predestination. Ha Jin's *Waiting* begins with this passage:

> Every summer Lin Kong returned to Goose Village to divorce his wife, Shuyu. Together they had appeared at the courthouse in Wujia Town many times, but she had always changed her mind at the last moment when the judge asked if she would accept a divorce. Year after year, they went to Wujia Town and came back with the same marriage license issued to them by the county's registry office twenty years before.[4]

Most American readers would be startled by this opening. How unthinkable, for a harmonious household to regularly get shaken up. Many agree this is the best-ever opening paragraph, like a mysterious, cool car picking them up to embark on a long journey in the stuffiest of summers. To readers in China, this passage isn't nearly as unexpected. It's merely everyday life to us. This is what we mean when we talk about escaping fate. Ha Jin's great accomplishment is illuminating how deeply an author can observe and bend to life and destiny. When I first read this passage more than a decade ago, I wasn't shocked, nor did I find it mundane. I don't know why, but it made me put down the book and sit in silence, all alone at home, for a very long time. I stared out the window at the chaos of the world, as if Ha Jin's acupuncture needle had slowly but steadily plunged into a neglected pressure point. A throbbing, tearful sorrow for Lin Kong and Shuyu welled up and flowed through my heart, refusing to be still. Silence arrived out of nowhere, and I was willing to drown in it, but I also yearned to rise from it. The same instant of hesitation, then perseverance, that I feel when diving into water holding my breath.

In 1984, I was hurrying urgently down the matrimonial road, weary, humiliated, and numb, until *she* halted my steps. I was twenty-six when I married, and by then my faith that I would escape my hometown had grown to the intensity of religious fervor. Wanting to have a family and a job in the city wasn't just my dream or the dream of my generation, or indeed that of each of several generations before us; I also saw it as a motivating force for the world to move toward civilization. This was the beginning of my life, the first goal of my writing career. When my fiction was published and I'd been promoted, I thought I had what it took to find a city wife, but in a mere three years I'd managed to cause hurt and be hurt in return. After getting sneered at and turned down by several city girls, I found that rejection was its own form of consolation. Inside me, exaggerated despair turned into constant silence and pain, simmering and scorching the rice of my youth. Yet I bore no hatred or rage for the city and its people; rather, I worked all the harder to chase after them. Then in late 1983, a friend introduced me to my wife. Not only was she from Kaifeng, a city, she was more beautiful and refined than all the girls I'd previously been set up with, which made me more hesitant yet accepting of our being together. I've never been able to work out whether there was hesitation or acceptance. I imagine this also puzzles her. In any case, we saw each other confusedly. I had no idea why she was holding back, or what she had accepted. My hesitation was that her parents, my would-be in-laws, had made it clear that they had three boys but only one girl, and after I left the army, they wanted us to remain in Kaifeng rather than allowing me to take their daughter to Luoyang or my hometown.

For all that I'd dreamt since I was a child of escaping to the city, the place where I truly hoped to settle was Luoyang in West Henan, which I'd thought of as the capital city since I first saw it in my teens, an ancient city only sixty kilometers from my hometown, not faraway Kaifeng. And so we hesitated over some things, and silently accepted others, including each other's hesitation. We wavered at the crossroads of our lives, as if a wind had arrived, but not knowing where to go, whirled and eddied around the junction. One day in 1984, my brother called me at my camp in Shangqiu to say our father had fallen seriously ill a few days ago. He'd summoned my brother to his bedside and told him that the asthma that had plagued him for years would make it difficult to survive the cold and desolation of winter. After a lifetime of hard work, three of his four children were married, but it pained him that his youngest son, Lianke, remained a bachelor.

If only Lianke could be married, he said, even if the frigid air took him from us, he'd go with a lighter heart.

My brother and I, a few hundred kilometers apart, were quiet for a while. I heard his ragged breath, sorrowful and helpless. He must be in one of the post office phone booths in Song County, West Henan. Maybe he detected the ineffectual distress of his little brother in East Henan. Neither of us said a word.

Just as it felt like the silence might explode, my brother slowly said, "Look, go talk it over with them, and if it's possible then you should get married. For our father's sake. You aren't getting any younger."

With that, he hung up.

In an office of Henan's Shangqiu Unit 33636, I heard the click. It sounded like a farmer feebly driving the hoe he'd used all his life into the soil at the end of the workday. The field and the hoe melded together, a single entity. I stared at the beads of my condensed breath on the receiver, then at the summer sky and trees in the courtyard outside the window. As I left the office, dismayed, I felt myself being forced to struggle free of the times and step into my destiny:

marriage. The great force of predestination wrapped around me. Not surrendering to it would be the greatest mistake of my life. The bugle signaled the end of the day, and the Klaxon summoned the division's cadres to the cafeteria.

I decided to skip dinner.

Not even going back to my dorm to get my stuff, I looked up at the vast dome of the heavens, then at the plains of East Henan beyond the red brick wall. I reached into my pocket for my wallet, a sheet of folded cardstock, and counted my money. Then I walked through the main gate of the camp.

Toward the train station.

I was getting married.

I was heading to Kaifeng, where I would say to my hesitant, accepting partner: Please marry me. I have to get married by the end of this year! That's what fate has arranged for me. My father's fate has decided mine. I wanted to tell her: If you say yes, we'll be like any other husband and wife in the world. If you refuse, let's part like a scattering flock of swallows, each flying in our own direction, and everything that passed between us will be no more than a random encounter in the street. To be honest, in that moment it didn't occur me to me to wonder whether marriage and the restrictions of our era belonged to me or to society and my family, or whether my decision would be violent or unfair to her, a threat or manipulation. With nothing in my heart but determination borne of destiny, I hurried decisively toward run-down Shangqiu Station.

Sprinting all the way, I managed to catch the bus.

At the other end, I leapt from the bus and ran to catch the one o'clock train. Back then, the trip from Shangqiu to

Kaifeng took about three hours, in the old green train of my memories. The seats were wooden slats, smooth and shiny from use. I bought a standing ticket and remained on my feet all the way. I can't recall what anxieties filled my mind as we sped through the wide, sandy plains of East Henan, nor whether I had any thoughts about hunger, poverty, escape, and struggle as we passed by the dunes of Lankao County, pillowy as steamed buns, famous thanks to the revolutionary example of Jiao Yulu. I'd read some books by then, and Julien Sorel had left a deep impression on me, just as the sickles we used back home at the wheat harvest had left scars on my body. How superior Julien's fate was to mine. I would never struggle to success as Julien once did. The distant city of Paris became a symbol of sacred love for me, a place I would never reach. The lives of the prosperous elite in Paris were gold cloth draped across the sky, out of my grasp, impossible to imagine. People like me might find shortcuts and thorny paths from the village to the city, generation after generation of youth striving to become one of the chosen, a striver with a room in the city, yet ours could never compare with the bitter battles that Julien fought. I had no idea that Julien's passion flowed in my veins too, that I possessed Julien's awareness of life and fate. I arrived in Kaifeng. There was the hutong with the Temple of the Chief Minister, as described in *The Water Margin*, and I waited there in the sunset for my sweetheart to return from work.

When she showed up, I would reveal my cards and lay out my proposal before her.

There she was, on her bicycle.

Spotting me at the hutong entrance, she froze for a second. Abruptly braking, she asked, as if nothing was out of the ordinary, "Are you in town for work?"

I didn't reply. As I'd pondered and planned all the way here, I stood in that hutong, a couple of paces from her, and told her that my father was ill; I wanted to get married; this was all for his sake. She stood facing me. Between us was her bicycle, ready to advance or retreat. I searched her face but couldn't tell if she was shocked or uneasy, happy or troubled. She worked at Kaifeng's electric vehicle factory, where she excelled as a lathe technician. Her gray-blue uniform blended into the dusk sky. We stood there for a while. Eventually, she said with great propriety, "I need to go home and talk it over with my parents."

And so she went home.

She left slowly, pushing the bicycle ahead of her as if it were the unknowable future, walking rather than getting back in the saddle. I watched as her shadow stretched dozens of paces ahead of her, and I called out, "I'll wait here for your answer!"

I don't know if shouting after her could be considered coercing or threatening, but it drew a line in the sand: this or that, nothing in between. She turned back to look at me, not nodding or saying anything, then walked away with deliberate steps, making her way slowly and carefully along the tightrope of her life.

I had a meal that served as both lunch and dinner at her street corner, Chuigutai Road. It took me more than thirty minutes to pay for a ticket, stand in line, collect my large bowl of stewed noodles, and grab a window seat. By then, she'd come back and was standing in the doorway searching for me. She hesitated a moment, blushing, then told me that her parents had agreed: We could get married, and if my father were to die, my mother could live in the city with us, so we'd be able to take care of her. Without waiting for me to respond, she looked left and right, then turned to go. As if I might have caused some sort of problem by lurking here, waiting to be betrothed. Or as if everything she'd just said was a pack of lies that she'd snuck out to comfort me with. Having said her piece, she hurried away from that small roadside restaurant. I was left gazing down the narrow, mottled hutong, watching her departing form, full of thanks and affection for our fate, hers and mine. I had no way to show my gratitude to her or how I loved my fate, unless I were to copy Raskolnikov in *Crime and Punishment*: "He knelt down in the middle of the square, bowed down to the earth, and kissed that filthy earth with bliss and rapture."[5]

As soon as she left, crystalline tears streamed from my eyes.

We were married on National Day that year, October 1, 1984.

That winter, not long after our wedding, my father left us and this world that he had always cherished, just as he had foreseen.

I've gained so much from being married to her. As for what she's gained or lost, how she's benefited or missed out—she has never thought or spoken about these things.

2
Big Sister, Second Sister, Sister-in-Law

Big Sister's Light Reading

In *Three Brothers*, I wrote about how my big sister was plagued by chronic pain in her bones since she was a child. Stabs of agony came from out of nowhere, making her want to smash her head into a wall. The rest of the time, she was peaceable and calm. She always had a book in her hands and enjoyed her light reading around the house or in the courtyard, where the sun was gentle and the light was soft. Sunlight would dapple Big Sister's face and book, and her waist-length braid, which she'd tossed behind her, kept falling forward onto her book. At these moments, the world was good. Birds sang in the trees. Our courtyard witnessed each sunrise and sunset and loyally kept the moon company as it rose and sank. Whenever it wasn't too hot or too cold, Big Sis would emerge from her room with a book and settle herself in a cozy nook near the doorway, beneath farming implements or strings of red chilis or garlic or the last golden ears of corn that we hadn't gotten round to cobbing all winter. The world quietened as she read; this scene could have been a sculpture or oil painting bestowed upon the world by God himself, perhaps titled *Quiet* or *Reading*, or more abstractly *Time* or *The Joy of Humanity*, or *The Final Pursuit of Humankind*.

In 2009, a colleague and I visited Málaga, Picasso's birthplace, where we saw the newly built Museo Picasso and had dinner with Picasso's elderly son. The most miraculous thing in the museum wasn't the paintings, but rather Picasso's very first sketch, made when he was twelve, of a girl standing in a field. Everyone said how talented he was, to draw so realistically at such a young age, but all I could think was, "This is nothing. The oil painting in my mind of Big Sis, *Young Woman Reading*, is so much better." Nothing about the drawing—the pencil strokes, the light, the entire conception—could compete with the picture in my head. During the banquet, when Picasso's son asked what I thought of it, I almost blurted out, "I don't see what the big deal is!"

In 2014, at Monet's garden in Giverny, I gazed at streams, water lilies, willow trees, and Japanese bridges. Everyone was taking photos and sighing over the paintings and scenery, but I felt Monet's creations weren't a patch on the landscapes in my mind, *Time* or *The Final Pursuit of Humankind*. Nor could they compete with the sights from my hometown locked in my memory: houses, courtyards, streets, fields, rivers, hills.

It's not that memory triumphs over time but rather that recollection is crueler and more magnificent than real life. Nothing in reality can compete with the wealth of material in our memories. When time transforms into remembrance, this act of creation makes it hyperreal. I can't forget the beauty of my big sister reading, perfectly still. I believe she found another world in her books, one more mystical, rare, and perfect than her actual surroundings.

I wanted to enter that world too.

Following in her footsteps, I took up reading in my spare time.

Her bedside table became my first library. Small as it was, it contained everything I could want. The first book I read was *Journey to the West*, which astounded me not because of the eighty-one ordeals that the pilgrims faced on their way to get the scriptures, but the idea that a stone could get pregnant and give birth. Next, I read *Three Family Lane*, *Red Sun*, *Red Crag*, *Red Flag*, *Behind Enemy Lines*, *The Railway Guerrillas*, *Song of Youth*, *The Big Knife*—pretty much all the revolutionary novels that were so in vogue at the time. The books by my sister's bed, with their idealized protagonists who didn't seek love and never feared death, were my first encounter with literature. I have no idea how many books I read then, nor did I have any sense of what literature actually was. I couldn't even have put a name to it. Nonetheless, I began to love it. Like my sister, I read day and night.

I often say the first foreign novel I read was Margaret Mitchell's *Gone with the Wind*, when I was twenty. But actually, my first foreign novel came to me without a title or cover, wrapped in brown paper. Big Sis handed it to me with great care, warning me not to lose it or get it dirty. Nothing she'd ever given me before deserved such reverence. This book must be important, from some special source. Obviously, this made me desperate to dig in. At lunchtime, I sat on the courtyard bench where Big Sis usually perched, a bowl of food in my hand, and started reading. Right away I was startled to learn that foreigners don't have names like us. Instead of Zhao or Qian or Sun, they were called Sergei or Anna or longer names I found impossible to remember. I wanted to rechristen them "Revolution Zhang" or "Red Flag Li," names that made sense to me. To be honest, I couldn't get into it. I wasn't really reading. From page one, those names kept me out. I stared at the page, wondering what I should rename Sergei, what surname to give Anna.

In the warm spring sunshine, I ate my lunch and pondered those names as if they were for my own children. Fine names such as Red Flag Li, Liberation Zhang, Spring Branch Zhao, Plum Blossom Sun. I soon finished eating but was still stuck on page one. Or maybe I got a little further, I don't remember. Leaving the book on the bench, I went to the kitchen with my bowl to get more rice. When I came back, the foreign novel was nowhere to be seen.

There wasn't a single soul in the courtyard.

The rest of my family had taken their food out to the village green, and none of them had come back for second helpings. Even if my parents or sisters had popped back in, they wouldn't have touched my book. The bright sunlight hadn't stolen it. The leaves were stuck to the tree branches, which surely hadn't bent over to help themselves to my book. The wind was too weak to even rustle the pages, let alone blow away an entire brick-thick book. I glared at the bench where I'd been sitting a moment ago. It remained silent and empty, not giving me a hint. Nothing underneath, nothing in its vicinity. No luck in the courtyard, no luck indoors. I even looked in the pigpen, in the backyard, all over the house, the entire heavens and earth. I looked everywhere, but the first foreign book I'd set eyes on was completely gone.

Big Sis was so angry, she slammed her bowl down on the table and glared at me with eyes like the world's largest grapes. She'd never looked so beautiful.

My parents and second sister helped to search. On the table. Under the table. All around the house. The chicken coop. The pigpen. But the book had utterly vanished. How very strange. It seemed that things kept happening in the world that should never happen. Traps laid for humanity, filled with absurdity. One might start believing in the existence of ghosts. The whole family was shaken by this bizarre disappearance. My mother's conclusion was, "This is providence telling you two not to waste your time reading. It ruins your eyes and wastes lamp oil." This is back when our household, like the rest of the village and, it seemed, the entire world, lit kerosene lamps at night. My father's view was deeper and more pessimistic: "I'm afraid the heavens confiscated the book so our family wouldn't produce a scholar."

Big Sis opened her eyes wide at this, as if God had revealed himself to her.

"It's fine," said my father. "Let them take our books, as long as they leave us behind."

He fretted that it wouldn't stop with books, that readers might be taken too.

I wasn't worried about the heavens. I couldn't stop thinking about how Big Sis would have to explain and pay back the person who'd lent her the book, a classmate who'd had it delivered from dozens of kilometers away, at great expense.

The rest of the day passed, and then the night. On the

evening of the second day, our sow had a litter. Eleven healthy piglets, dull yellow-red like gold bars. She'd never had this many, and even the ones she had often died young. With this litter, my family saw a bright ray of hope. Everyone kept saying ecstatically they'd skip a meal if it meant the sow could eat better. More importantly, and more enigmatically, when the sow got up to eat from the trough, my mother looked at her disheveled sleeping spot, with straw and branches strewn everywhere. In this birthing bed she'd improvised for herself, amid the vegetal matter, was the foreign book I'd lost.

The brown paper wrapping had toothmarks where the sow had picked it up, and it was a little stained with fluids from the birth. Didn't all of this, at some level, point to the connection between reading, writing, and existence? A secret code of some sort?

Big Sister's Braid

My elder sister was famous for the beauty of her braided hair. Everyone in our village knew of its gleaming darkness, its thickness, its length. She kept it smooth and neat, hanging down her back or over her shoulder on her chest. Simply ravishing. An angel of the countryside. When she walked down the street, passersby would cry out, "Wow! Look at her hair!"

I was proud of my sister's hair. Often, I would look at it and think, "Just imagine how much you could sell that for."

Back then, my main approach to girls was judging if their hair was pretty or not.

The fifth of every month was market day in our village. Every year, after the rainy season but before the start of summer, there'd be one temple fair after another, and people would come from all around, gathering in the spring warmth on the north bank of our river. There'd be Beijing or Henan opera—often *The Legend of the Red Lantern* or *Shajiabang*. The performances weren't anything special, but the crowd made things lively, like bees around fragrant flowers. One year, on the eighteenth day of the third month, I saw a visiting troupe from Luoyang perform the Beijing opera *The Legend of the Red Lantern*. The actress playing Li Tiemei had such a long, thick braid that the audience exclaimed at it. I came to the show because of that braid, but when I shoved my way to the front of the crowd, I saw it was shorter than my sister's, and clearly fake—a rope of hair, thick as a human wrist, tied to her real hair with a red ribbon at her neck.

I hurried home to tell Big Sis that Li Tiemei's braid was nothing special, just a wig.

I got back around noon.

As soon as I stepped in the front gate, I saw my entire family drinking soda from brownish-red bottles around the size of Tsingtao beers, with beads of condensation clinging to them. Everyone had a bottle to themselves, and on their faces were smiles of contentment. Father, Mother, Brother and Second Sister threw their heads back to guzzle their sodas, then held the bottles up to the sunlight. This was a surprise—since when did we have soda at home? Big Sis emerged from the house with a soda in one hand and a bucket of cold water in the other, and in the bucket another bottle was bobbing around. She set down the bucket in front of me, took the final bottle from its bath and handed it to me. Only then did I notice her braid was gone, and her hair only reached halfway down her neck. It made her look older than her fourteen or fifteen years, like a village girl of marriageable age. I thought she was even more beautiful than before. Her smile as she drank her soda had the same relaxed satisfaction as the rest of my family, a slowly spreading happiness.

She had traded her hair for these sodas.

She'd seen someone in the street selling soft drinks, and it felt like when human beings first discovered that the fruit hanging from trees was sweet. She had cut her hair off and sold it to the junk store, earning herself thirty-two cents. The sodas were five cents a bottle, so she'd bought six—one for each family member—leaving her with two cents. We drank our sodas, and then there was nothing left of my sister's long hair.

This was our first taste of soda. It was ambrosial, the nectar of the gods.

Big Sis also gave me the remaining two cents, enough at the time for a small egg or a couple of candies.

Official Status

1.

Clouds roil and calm again. The sun rises and sets.

After Big Sis graduated from middle school, she was lucky enough to find a job teaching elementary school.

I was still at school myself. Later, I dropped out of high school to work, and she went on teaching. I joined the army, and still she taught. Eventually, I attained cadre status and people started calling me an "author," while she remained a teacher at a village elementary school. Time flows on, more forcefully and relentlessly than any river, like a cloud that has never been battered by wind. Many rivers have run dry, but time has never stopped. I have a clear sense of how I got to where I am today, but I don't have the faintest idea how my sisters, sister-in-law, or mother ended up where they are. In my memory, their lives do not consist of links in a chain but rather leap from one event to the next. If not for those incidents I remember, I'd feel as if their existences contained no time at all.

While I was in the army, Big Sis got married to a man from the village. I only found out the next time I came back for a family visit. My mother told me, and I gaped at her as if our home had been burgled. My heart was completely empty. A pitch-black abyss opened up before my eyes. Big Sis was gone. My brother-in-law might as well have gouged out my heart. I asked my mother why she hadn't written to let me know, and she said there was no point, it's not like I could have come back for the wedding. She was placidly rinsing vegetables, and for the first time I read something in her calm demeanor: That's how life is; you're cramped in on all sides, yet it keeps turning like a waterwheel.

As I ate lunch with my parents and Second Sis, I kept feeling something was missing from the house, something we'd been unable to hold on to, so we had to bear the loss in silence. That evening, Big Sis came to see me. She was pregnant. Already she was waddling, and she rubbed her swollen legs when she sat down. I didn't know what to say or ask her.

All of a sudden, my elder sister had become a stranger, no closer than a neighbor. Trying to regain our closeness, I thought of offering to take over her teaching duties so she could rest at home. Then I overheard her asking Second Sis to sub for her. Second Sis nodded yes, and they began discussing everything she needed to know to teach elementary school. Their animated discussion filled the house. My parents sat watching and listening. In the last few years, the electric lights of civilization had finally reached our home, and high-voltage power lines had appeared on the road outside. Green transformer boxes with curved tubes stood all around, including on the vacant lot to the west of our house. In honor of my return, my mother had swapped the fifteen-watt bulbs for forty-watt ones. They blazed away, bringing beauty to every corner. I sat there, bathed in light, feeling like an outsider. Now that I was in the army, I couldn't do anything useful for my family.

I sat there numbly, in the light.

After a few more days of numbness, I returned to my unit.

By the time of my next family visit the following year, both my brother and my other sister had gotten married too. Now it was just me and my parents. Unlike other people, I didn't feel they'd suddenly gotten older—rather, it seemed they'd never been young. They'd always been elderly strivers, not stopping their work even when they sat down—my mother had her sewing, my father shucked corn, cleaned his farm tools, or patched a bamboo or willow basket. They thought it was a sin to sit there doing nothing. Endless labor was the only proper way for a farmer to live, the only thing that gave them meaning. Big Sis and her husband dropped by with their one-year-old daughter. When I took the infant from my brother-in-law, Big Sis told her to call me "uncle," and the sallow little girl cried out, "Uncle!"

I froze.

I wasn't surprised that a one-year-old child could speak, but it felt as if something Big Sis took away when she got married had now been restored to me.

I was an "uncle."

I had become an "uncle."

Was this life?

Yes, this is what life was!

My mother had stoked a huge fire, and my father was sitting upwind so the smoke wouldn't aggravate his asthma. It kept threatening to snow, dry and cold and gloomy, as if we were all in a gigantic cave. All of humanity in this cavernous space. Roaming around and trying to find a way out, unable to escape. Trapped since time immemorial in this chasm. As we roasted ourselves by the fire, Big Sis and her husband hesitantly told me something: The school was starting to give official status to some of the community teachers. Big Sis was from the oldest batch of community teachers and had been given model educator status at her appraisal each year. Her classes invariably got the highest grades in the whole school. They hoped I could have a word with the relevant county officials to consider her for official status when the time came.

To bolster her daughter's credentials, Mother mentioned that she'd collapsed at the lectern a couple of times out of sheer fatigue, got carried out on a stretcher, and showed up to teach the next day as if nothing had happened.

I stared at Big Sis in surprise.

She flushed and looked down.

After hearing that she'd fainted twice at the "lectern"—which was just a raised mound of dirt—I knew what I could do for her. I would more than pay her back for the soda and two cents she'd sold her hair to give me. I immediately said yes, I would speak with the county chief the very next day. I had a bit of "fame" by then, and I'd met the county chief before, so everyone thought my ugly mug would be received as if it were the radiant full moon. They rejoiced. Surely a word from me would elevate my sister from community to official teacher, just like that. My brother-in-law and mother got excited too, and even my father's wan, sickly face was now glowing and ruddy.

The next day, I got the bus to the county seat and went to see my brother, who was working at the post office, to tell him what was going on. By calling from the post office phone, he managed to quickly get connected to the county government office. It didn't take long for the county chief to agree to see me. My brother gave me a lift. I was already an experienced writer in the army and had no problem speaking confidently and clearly to my superior officers, reporting on all sorts of things, yet the prospect of stepping into the county government building and facing the chief in those magnificent settings left me feeling all kinds of unease. I would be asking the supervisor of the entire county for a personal favor. His office was on the second floor. As I entered, I noticed it was larger than my commanding officer's. Much larger. Dazzlingly bright too, as if the sun itself emanated from this building.

The conversation went incredibly smoothly. It made me believe that when God said, *Let there be light*, there was indeed light. He said, *Let the land be parted from the waters*, and so it was, and there were seas, and there were hills, plains, and wildernesses. It was ten in the morning when I walked into the county chief's office, and I was back out less than fifteen minutes later. I went in blushing, uncertain where to sit, accepting a glass of water poured for me by the county chief himself, and began an awkward recitation of my big sister's circumstances and request. Unexpectedly, he breezily agreed, with no sign of hesitation, and even made a note of her name on his desk calendar.

"It's rare for our county to produce such a gifted individual. I'll make sure I do this for you!" he repeated a couple of times as I stood to leave.

When I emerged from the building, my brother made me tell him everything and exclaimed, "That's great!" He took me and his wife to a restaurant for a delicious meal.

I got home to find my sister and brother-in-law waiting for news. I told them what had happened, and it was as if we'd won the lottery. Such excitement and high emotion. We had another delicious meal: griddled flatbreads, stir-fried greens, egg-drop noodle soup. With my father's medical expenses, they could only afford such indulgences two or three times a month. But that day, we gorged ourselves.

Then I returned to my unit.

Sometime later, a letter arrived from my sister. A week after I'd returned to my unit, the county chief had been transferred. Another batch of community teachers had been given official status. Some were older than her, others had only been in their positions for a couple of years. Some had rotten personalities and weren't very good at teaching yet had somehow snagged promotions.

Once again, her name was missing from the list.

2.

From this point on, attaining official status became the entire purpose of my sister's existence, and also a test of my abilities: Would I be able to bring about this thing for my family? Big Sis refused to take time off even when she was ill. After her second baby, she hurried back to the podium before her maternity leave was up. On my annual visit home, I'd hoped for a visit from a county cadre, or thought I could find some excuse to have a meal with the county chief and his bureau heads. For a long time, my failure to help my sister made me wonder what the purpose of writing was. I trusted it a little less.

The good thing is, hard work will get noticed—it truly will—by those who are paying attention. I seemed to have become a real writer. It was easy for me to get my pieces accepted by magazines, and I frequently earned more from this than from my actual salary. I began to publish books. Now I could present people with my own novels as gifts, ostentatiously signing my name on the flyleaf. These books made their winding way to the county seat and turned me into a writer who could truly achieve anything. And so it was that one night, I was getting ready for bed at the family quarters in Kaifeng camp when someone from the county government office barged in, introduced himself, presented me with the many local treats he'd brought with him, took a seat, and began ceremoniously holding forth about reform and opening up, and the changes and accomplishments in this county over the last few years. He hoped I would come back soon for a visit, to write an essay that could appear in the *Henan Daily*. Naturally, this top-notch cadre from my hometown didn't forget to ask if my family had any problems that needed solving, anything at all the county could help with, so they'd have the chance to show their concern for us all.

I thought about my sister. He'd driven hundreds of kilometers to Kaifeng just to ask me to write a piece for the local paper. I agreed to a visit soon.

Of course, my itinerary was arranged for me.

Writing is a glorious, illuminating thing, like a stormy sky clearing and a rainbow springing from your page. My visit lasted maybe two or three days. The deadline was urgent as a volcanic eruption: The piece needed to be published by a particular date. I think we had two weeks total for writing and editing, which meant I didn't even have time to go see my mother. I stayed at a hotel in the county seat, and after I'd seen what I needed to see, I phoned my brother and said Big Sis should get her promotion, no problem, the county chief was practically thumping his chest when he agreed. Then I rushed back to the camp one blazing twilight, ready to write my article.

Half a month later, "Springtime in My Hometown," both an essay and a piece of reportage, was printed in the *Henan Daily*, taking up more than half a page. They hadn't changed a word. Prominent as the sun and moon. My sister would get promoted for sure—this was quid pro quo, and I'd held up my end of the bargain. Another month passed, and the county chief was abruptly transferred. A lateral transfer, without promotion. When I returned the following year, the cadre who'd summoned me back from Kaifeng was standing on the main road of the county seat, smiling grimly as he informed me that the day after my article was published, a provincial working group happened to arrive in our county. A copy of the newspaper was placed in each of their hotel rooms. It was already known that the secretary of the county's party committee was being transferred out, and the county chief was being considered to replace him. That's why he was so insistent that the article be published that day: Having the working group see it would be quite a boost for his promotion.

Even with this boost, he failed to secure the party secretary's position. Instead, he was sent away too.

Afterward, I often wondered if my shamelessly, ridiculously fawning words had ended up hurting the county chief's chances.

3.

I was in utter despair about my big sister's situation.

I began to believe that when it came to literature, as long as you cleared the bar of "aesthetics," the rest was just grit, air, and water, mixed together and baked into a loaf of bread. Kneading sand into a length of rope. Another year passed, and once again I was back home for the Spring Festival. The county chief and secretary both came by to say hello, and as they left they called out, "Lianke—if you need anything, just let us know!" All our neighbors heard this, and as soon as the officials were gone, they crowded into our home to say the county was laying a new road, and I ought to have a word with them to extend a branch up to my front door, which would mean the twenty-odd households on our hutong could have a paved road rather than a dirt track.

What ended up happening was I put my hand into my pocket and paid the workers to do a little overtime to extend the road down our hutong. The neighbors were delighted: They no longer had to wade through mud whenever it rained or snowed. My mother too was happy that she no longer needed to worry about tripping when she came home after dark. Sometime after this, my sister bought the most expensive liquor and cigarettes available in our town and trotted down the paved road of the hutong to our home, where she plonked the booze, smokes, and a dozen of her teaching awards down in front of me. "Lianke, I know you're thin-skinned, I know your words are precious. You'd never lower yourself to ask the county officials for anything. So for the last time, just hand these gifts to the county chief and secretary. If you do that, even if I never get official status, I'll accept my fate."

If I thought she hadn't brought enough, she added, she'd go back to the high street to get more. My mother agreed with her. If I was willing to spend thousands getting a paved road for our hutong, why not open my mouth in front of the new county chief and secretary? Would speaking a few words make the lips fall off my face?

My second sister took their side too. As did the wind and grass and the leaves on the trees. The sky, the earth, the universe itself. Not one person felt my big sis had said or done anything untoward. It was October, the season of harvest and fruitfulness. I'd now spent six years trying to obtain official status for my sister, getting through three county chiefs and three party secretaries. Big Sis was now a middle-aged lady, and I still hadn't resolved her problem. Meanwhile, two or three community teachers were being granted official status each year. Some were more qualified; others couldn't hold a candle to her. At this point, it felt like the question wasn't whether Big Sis could be promoted but whether I had the ability to see this through. Whether all my hard work would amount to anything. But it also felt as if all I had to do was persevere, and the fog would clear, revealing the far shore of her life. The wind and thunder held their tongues, while birds twittered to themselves. People in Africa have African problems, people in Europe have European problems. And in my village, we have village problems. Every world is different. Yet a different world is still a world, and the human beings in it are still people.

This time round, I called on a good friend, a reporter at the *Luoyang Daily*. He'd mentioned he was close to the county chief and party secretary. We bought more liquor and cigarettes, and the next day, we headed to the county seat. After lunch, during naptime, we barged into the party secretary's home. My journalist friend announced that we were here to present the secretary with some gifts, set them down firmly on the table, and presented the party secretary with my sister's teaching CV and a list of her many accomplishments. Isn't someone like this amply qualified to receive official status? he demanded. And if not, how come so many lesser teachers have been promoted over her head, while she waits empty-handed year after year?

The party secretary gaped at him, dumbfounded. My friend forced him to pick up the phone and find out what was going on.

Next, we went to the county chief's house and followed exactly the same procedure. Said all our lines again. Crucially, when the party secretary refused to accept the cigarettes and alcohol, my reporter friend tossed them next to the trash can outside his front door, right in front of him, and led me away in a perfect performance of rage. When the county chief said the same thing, my friend once again threw—actually, placed—them on the ground next to the trash can.

Three months later, the county officials wrote and Big Sis phoned to let me know she was receiving official status as a teacher. She'd started working at the school when she was seventeen, and now at the age of forty-eight, she was finally a fully fledged educator. Beneath the dark sky and on the yellow earth, human existence is desolate. Don't ask if it's better for a river to flow shallow or deep, as long as it flows. At lunchtime, I sprinted from the office to the family quarters, my feet barely touching the ground. I told my wife that my sister's problem had been resolved. She stood frozen, holding the rice she'd just finished rinsing, and echoed, "Resolved." Then she set aside the rice, rolled up her sleeves, and prepared to make dumplings.

We had a celebratory meal of pot stickers.

I ate too much, and all afternoon my stomach felt full, which only made me want to smile. A few months later, my wife and I went back home, and my sister came to see us. After sharing all the happy news about our family and the village, she said she shouldn't have given me such a hard time. She was official now, but so were the other seven or eight community teachers at their school. Every community teacher in our county had been promoted that year. It was the last year of the program, and anyone who didn't have any issues had received official status. Everyone in the whole of China, promoted in a single stroke.

After she'd told us this, my sister, my wife, and I stood in the autumnal dusk of the courtyard, looking at the sky, looking at the ground, looking at the world and the humanity around us. I laughed and said to Big Sis, "So I ran around a bit and delivered some presents, and that made your promotion more assured. If I hadn't done that, maybe there'd be a single school with a single teacher who didn't have official status, and that person would be you."

She thought about it and laughed too. "That's true!"

Now we were all laughing. A family's laughter, like a warm ocean.

Depression

My second sister is an empiricist. No matter what, she will only make judgments based on experience and the evidence of her senses.

She believes that people live for their goals. Without a goal, why would anyone do this or that? Goals are the beginning and end of all human behavior, she claims. That's her philosophy of life. One time, she applied her framework to our big sister's entire existence and motivation. Big Sis loved her job and worked hard at it because it's better to be a teacher than a farmer. She strived for honors and made herself a role model in her quest for official status. As for why she continued being so assiduous afterward, that was because fully fledged teachers were divided into levels, just as there were four different tiers of professors. Each time you went up a level, your salary increased by a hundred yuan.

Having delivered her analysis, Second Sis said with some concern, "Big Sis is retiring soon, which means her life will soon have no motivation or goal. It'll be empty. And once it's hollowed out, the sky will fall down on her existence."

Unfortunately, Second Sis got that right.

The year she turned fifty, Big Sis returned home with her certificate of commendation and rosette. Before dust could gather on either of these, she'd already been on several excursions with tour groups from the town and the county seat and was starting to realize that the only meaningful thing in her life was standing at the school podium.

She now had too much time on her hands. In our village, women only had a few activities available to them: playing mahjong, gossiping, doing calisthenics on the village green. Unfortunately, Big Sis didn't know how to do any of these things. She began feeling a persistent discomfort and took to visiting the hospital every few days, where they invariably found some minor ailment that put her at risk. For instance, if her throat was inflamed, the doctor would say this had to be treated today, or tomorrow it might turn into cancer of the esophagus. If she felt dizzy, that could be a spinal issue or something to do with her blood pressure, but the doctor would say blood flow to her heart might be constricted, and she needed a CT scan, or MRI, or they had to keep her overnight for observation. Sure enough, her heart rate increased, which meant she had arrhythmia, or else her left atrium had this, her right ventricle had that. She trusted the doctors as fully as she trusted the Party. She believed every one of their hints and guesses. Surely, they and the hospital only had her best interests at heart. She believed the packets and sachets of medicine, both Western and traditional, would cure her of every illness, but they only gave her relief for three to five days, a week at most. When she wasn't better in ten days, she'd panic and see a different doctor at a different hospital, and this other doctor would go through the whole sequence of taking her pulse, asking her questions, putting her through a battery of tests and charging yet more fees. Eventually, they'd refute the previous doctors and prescriptions and give her a different set of meds and treatments.

In this way, my big sister, who only used to walk between her home and the elementary school, now expanded her itinerary to take in the town, the county seat, Luoyang, and eventually Beijing, as she sought out ever more hospitals. She burned through her pension, as if she'd spent more than thirty years teaching for the sake of handing over her money at the counters of various hospitals. My mother said, sympathetically, "It's a good thing your sister gets a pension, otherwise how would she pay for her treatment?" Sharply, my brother retorted, "If she didn't have the cash, she'd stop seeing doctors. When she has nothing in her hands but air, maybe she'll stop being ill."

Second Sis could only sigh, having foreseen this long ago. Big Sis's husband, son, and daughter-in-law couldn't understand why she wasn't living the serene, stable, and comfortable life they'd envisioned for her after retirement.

Why was she running herself ragged? They urged her to stop her blind faith in doctors, to stop spending all her time in hospitals. They quarreled and Big Sis grew resentful that they didn't want her to get treatment, which meant they didn't care about her health. She constantly complained and threw tearful tantrums. In a short span of time, she'd gone from being a respectable teacher to a figure as pitiable as Auntie Xianglin from Lu Xun's "New Year's Sacrifice." This went on until my mother, brother, and other sister came to realize that Big Sis really was ill. She'd spent her time at school putting far too much energy into being a model teacher and getting official status, into her students, her lectern, her community duties, her schedule. After retirement, the ground fell out from beneath her feet and she had no reason to go on living, which drove her into sadness and anxiety. Neither we nor the hospitals took this seriously, until it worsened and left her with chronic depression.

Second Sis

Let's talk about my second sister.

She was once known as "Radish," though that's top secret these days. Even her son, daughter-in-law, and grandchildren have no idea. How did she end up with that nickname? The most encyclopedic account would be unable to answer that question. That's the nature of history—it forgets more than it remembers. If it were the other way round, we'd end up so paralyzed by the weight of recollection that we wouldn't be able to stir an inch.

I too am better at forgetting, but I do remember where

Second Sis got her nickname. When I was six and she was eight, our schoolhouse was also a temple. At the year-end exams, I got scores of sixty-one and sixty-two in math and Chinese, which of course meant I could move on to the next grade. That's no small matter. Even when the entire class moved up a grade, many of my classmates would get full marks in both subjects, as if the gods were helping them. After all, there were many gods of all hues painted on the walls and pillars of our classroom.

The gods never helped me.

Nor did Second Sis.

Not only did she refuse to help me, she told my parents that I got the lowest scores in the entire class, in fact in my entire year. If I let her get away with this, what would she do next? Already my mother was glaring at me with such a frosty look, you'd have thought I wasn't her child at all. The north wind rose, freezing the sky and land, setting its icy feet down in our courtyard. My mother's reproachful eyes were colder than winter. Way below freezing. Maybe a hundred degrees below. How else would I still feel her frigid stare, even today? How would I remember, a half century later, why my sister was called Radish?

No, I couldn't let her get away with that.

I'd have left her alone if she'd left me alone, but now it was time for payback. At dinner time, I lurked outside our front door with my bowl, and when she emerged with her food I leapt at her and yelled, "Radish, radish, big fat radish!" What happened next? Both tragedy and comedy, as I passed the baton of grievance from my heart to hers. She was so startled that she dropped her bowl, and the humiliation of being called a radish made her blush bright red. She knelt on the ground and began sobbing.

From then on, that nickname was my weapon against Second Sis. Whenever I needed to fight back, yelling "Radish" a few times did the trick.

As a young boy and little brother, I had morality and destiny on my side, just as a tree branch holds the apple aloft so the apple can bask in the warmth and yearning of those who look upon it. Only an idiot would pay attention to the kindness and support that the branch gives the fruit. As for the branch, all it can hope for is that when the apple departs, it doesn't curse its former host for not providing enough.

But how could you not look back and curse? My sister's nickname is Radish.

Work Points

In a moment of carelessness, I got older.

Now I could join my parents on the production brigade, heading into the fields with hoe and shovel to become one with the yellow earth. The wheat harvest was the most intense, exhausting time of year. The farmers and cadres pulled in everyone capable of movement to scythe and glean. The sun blazed so fiercely you could hear the tree-tops screeching as they got scorched. Amid those shrieks, the brigade had to hurry to gather the wheat while also tallying everyone's work points.

Men in their prime started each day with ten points. Those who showed themselves to be weak or sneaky had their dignity trimmed to nine points.

Women of a certain age started the day with eight. Seven, if they were feeble or lazy.

Schoolchildren started with five or six points. Six was reserved for the most outstanding youths. Our brigade was the wealthiest in the whole village and paid out 12 cents for every ten work points. Six points were worth 7.2 cents, the cost of three eggs. I aspired to be one of those fine young people who got awarded six points each day and invited the fierce sun to witness me gathering wheat.

The sun was a blaze of yellow. The fields were golden with wheat. And we were all covered in muddy yellow grime. In this wash of yellow, the adults scythed and the kids followed behind, gathering the ears of wheat, scanning every inch of ground that had been cleansed by the blades.

Wild rabbits scampered amid the stubble.

Sparrows swooped down, delighted at the banquet laid before them.

The schoolchildren set to work. To make sure the brigade leader and other adults noticed me and awarded me six points, I yelled "Radish" at Second Sis and snatched a fresh basket from her hands, then bent over the fields allocated to me, not straightening up for a couple of hours, scooping up one fallen ear after another. The sun rose higher, and I'd filled half a basket. Even higher, and my bamboo basket was almost full. As it reached its peak, the uncle and auntie ahead of me had reached the far end of the field with their scythes, but I was lagging far behind and had only gleaned two-thirds of the ears. Meanwhile, my neighbors and schoolmates, all around my age, were managing to more or less keep up with their adults.

I began to feel uneasy.

So anxious I could have pissed myself.

For the sake of six work points and 7.2 cents, I almost peed my pants. Just as the pressure on my bladder grew intolerable, I realized the field before me was bare, picked so clean you'd have thought a flock of sparrows had just passed by. Not even a grain remained.

Startled, I straightened up.

Second Sis was walking toward me. As she hastily tipped her half-full basket into mine, she murmured, "Quick, go report to the brigade leader."

Then she ducked aside.

She'd worked extra fast, clearing her own field so she could help with mine. I rushed to the brigade leader with my overflowing basket. When he saw how much I had, he was so delighted that he gave me an affectionate kick in the rump. That year, Second Sis and I both received six work points every day, and at the end of the year we received 7.2 cents for each day we'd worked, exactly enough to buy three eggs.

From then on, I stopped calling my second sister Radish.

Hauling Coal

Back in the day, families that were doing well cooked their meals over a coal fire, while those doing less well used firewood. This was the most accurate gauge of a household's means. If your son or daughter was looking for a mate and you wanted to see if a prospective fiancé or fiancée was thriving or struggling, it wasn't enough just to look at their home. Thatched or tile roof? Mud, brick, or stone walls? Those alone weren't a true measurement of wealth. You also had to see whether their family burned coal or wood when it came time to cook.

My family was doing okay: We had a tile-roofed house, and sometimes we used coal, especially at Spring Festival time. The only place to buy coal was Tall Mountain Mine, forty kilometers away along a hilly road. Second Sis and I went with the other villagers to haul coal. This was a solemn, ceremonial moment. This meant we'd grown up and could carry out a task that only a worker could do. My asthmatic father no longer had to brave the chill and the north wind, panting like a sick ox. Nor did we have to beg someone else to get up while it was still dark and go fetch coal for us.

The night was half gone, and dawn still hours away, when the rooster's cry stabbed through the village. We got out of bed, fetched the wagon, threw on our jackets, slung the rations our mother had prepared the night before over the wagon shaft, prodded the wheels hard to make sure they were fully inflated, and placed the air cannister in the cart. Finally, we went to our father's bedside so he could repeat the instructions he'd already given us: "On your way back, when you're going uphill, be sure to move in an S-shape so the gradient isn't so steep; if the path is too narrow to move in an S, wait for someone else to come by, and ask that uncle to lend you a hand. Most importantly, you'll be buying 500 pounds of coal, but as you're loading the cart, be sure to keep hammering the loose coal with your shovel, or one of you could load while the other stomps on the coal. If the scale shows you have 550 pounds instead of 500, then they'll remove some, cursing the whole while, but if you've compacted the coal they may only get rid of 20 or 30 pounds before giving up, so you'll leave with more than you paid for."

Such a mystical life experience. Second Sis and I set off, hugging this exciting secret to our chests.

It was the last lunar month of the year, the night was cold and deep, and the sky was a glass bowl held upside down far above us. Dogs barked, sounding like dogs, and roosters crowed, sounding like roosters. Our footsteps beneath that sky did not sound human, though, but like knocking on the wooden door of life. We were with five or six other wagons, each pulled by a single person. Only ours had two youths. Our fellow villagers were afraid we'd fall behind, so they made sure we were in the middle of the convoy. Worried that our legs weren't up to walking almost a hundred kilometers, whenever we reached level ground, someone would let us couple our wagon to theirs and hitch a ride, conserving our energy. Around fifteen kilometers in, we reached a place called Minggao, where we turned from the main road onto a dirt track. The villagers told us to take turns, one of us pulling the wagon while the other rested their legs, to reduce the distance each of us walked. That would leave us with more energy for the return journey with a full load. As we trudged through the darkness, some people sang while others abruptly let out a shriek from time to time, for some reason.

We passed one village after another.

Just before dawn, we arrived at the coal mine.

There was already a long line ahead of us.

We hadn't seen any other coal haulers on the way here, but as we approached the dark mountains of coal, we saw cars and tractors waiting, and even more wagons, as if they'd been spewed up by the earth itself. Chaos and cacophony. Some people had gotten here especially early and were wreathed in smoke as they grilled food. All the faces around us were dark with dirt and coal dust. Some had already loaded their carts and were setting off joyously. Their carts were loaded with not just powdered coal but also gleaming nuggets and kernels. An experienced villager told me and Second Sis that we should go for the larger chunks when we were loading our cart. Those burned longer and better—refined food, compared to the coarse rations of coal powder. We nodded, inched our wagon forward, and started devouring the griddled flatbreads our mother had made specially for us.

The flatbreads were stuffed with scallions, so fragrant it felt as if the whole world was suffused with the aroma of alliums and wheat. We lit a fire and boiled water by the side of the road, and it tasted sweet and tepid, as if life itself were a dish of fried pocket eggs sprinkled with sugar. Everything was good and beautiful, fresh and warm, while time sped on, hot and fast. The sun had barely risen when we got to the front of the line.

The shovels provided by the mine were twice as large as the ones at home. I was stronger than Second Sis, so I was in charge of loading the cart, while she scrabbled around the coal heap for larger pieces. When I got tired, she took over while I jumped into the cart to stomp on the coal. We quickly filled our own bamboo cart and even had time to help the other villagers. When everyone was done, we went to the weighing area and handed over our tickets to show we'd already paid. I can't remember how much coal the two middle-aged men removed from our cart. One of them kept an eye on the scale while the other shoveled. One of them looked at us and said, "Oh wow, you're just kids!" With each scoop of coal he removed, our hearts ached. After a while, Second Sis said to the shoveler, "Please stop, or we won't even have five hundred pounds left." He glanced at the man at the scale, who nodded. Before setting down his shovel, he tossed a scoop back onto the cart.

We pulled our wagon off the scale.

At a nearby vacant area, we waited for the others to be done. As everyone compared their loads, they noticed ours had a large scoop taken out of the center and worried we might not have as much as we paid for, that the workers might have removed too much. It felt as if someone had scooped away a chunk of our flesh. But it was gone, and there was no help for it; we just had to put up with the agony. Then Second Sis walked over to a nearby fire pit and returned with a heap of coal nuggets cradled in her jacket—when they put out the fire, they hadn't salvaged the unburned coal. By reclaiming it, Second Sis made up for the anxiety of not having a full load, and we felt the soothing satisfaction of not having been cheated. Now our convoy could set off.

Uphill, downhill.

Downhill, uphill.

It felt as if there wasn't a single level stretch of road all the way home, just as no one's life can be perfectly smooth the whole time. I held on to the shafts while my sister pulled a rope to the side. We started out in a row, but the stronger, swifter ones among us soon took the lead, and then our convoy scattered. We no longer knew if we were in front of or behind the others. We pulled with our heads down, not saying a word. After maybe fifteen or twenty kilometers, we felt the grayish-yellow sun directly overhead—noontime, it seemed. We stopped by the side of the road, and I went in search of stones to build a firepit, while Second Sis set off with an aluminum pot to fetch water from the closest village. By the time she got back, I'd gathered enough wood to start a fire.

Our lunch was noodle soup, to which we added the cabbage leaves our mother had chopped and packed for us, with salt and lard nestled between them. Second Sis did the cooking, and it was as tasty as New Year dumplings. We sat on a rock by the side of the road, each holding an enamel bowl, gazing at the vast, empty world as we ate. The light gradually dimmed, and it felt as if the rest of our lives were spread out before us. Up ahead, another villager finished lunch and started moving again, followed by a dog. Someone else overtook us, their eyes passing right over us.

When we were almost done, Second Sis asked me out of nowhere, "Lianke, what do you want to do when you grow up?"

I stared at her, confused about why she was asking this and how I ought to respond. The northern winter was harsh and desolate, and if you spilled water onto the road it froze immediately. The sprouting wheat stalks in the fields were black from frostbite, making you worry they wouldn't come back to life in the spring. In this cruel cold, although the hot noodle soup had warmed our bodies, our insides still felt hollowed out, as if our souls had nothing to rest on, as if we were adrift in space, and no matter how hard we scrabbled, our feet wouldn't find the ground. Later, when I learned about ancient Greek mythology, I was touched and saddened by the fate of Antaeus, who died when he was no longer in contact with the earth. Back then, all I had was ignorance and emptiness within me, a borderless expanse in my heart. I stared blankly at my sister, waiting for her to explain my future to me.

She'd given it some serious thought. "You're a boy, so you should try your best to leave home."

I went on staring at her, uncomprehending. My bowl remained frozen in midair.

"If there's no other way, you can join the army. Once you get promoted to cadre, you won't have to suffer like this."

She didn't say anything further, and I felt as if I was scanning the horizon for my future, unable to see where it was. Amid this wilderness of unknowing, we set off again. Although there were two of us, we somehow weren't as strong as a single adult. It didn't occur to us that we were allowed to arrive home a little later; we pulled the wagon along in a frenzy, as if our home would vanish if we slowed down. It was late afternoon by the time we finally turned from the dirt track back onto the paved road. Second Sis and I changed positions; now she was between the shafts and I was pulling the rope. She looked like a sheep trying to pull a horse carriage, and my heart twinged for her.

Turns out you get down a road one step at a time, and you haul a load uphill one shoulder at a time.

Hill roads aren't just there for people to walk up; they also allow you to drag a cart of coal up like a horse or ox. When the wind rose, we worried it would blow away the coal dust, so Second Sis chipped through the ice in the gutter and filled our cooking pot, then scattered bowlfuls of water over the cart. At the front of the cart, where the coal was piled against a curve of woven bamboo, I placed a couple of blocks of ice. We started moving again. As our father had instructed us, we moved in an S-shape when going uphill, and where the road was too narrow, we waited till an uncle or auntie came along who could help.

As we toiled, afternoon faded away and evening arrived. The ramrod-straight poplar trees waved their branches in the air, beckoning us, but we didn't so much as turn our heads in acknowledgement. Our eyes were fixed to the ground and we kept hauling, kept walking. Now I was between the shafts, now Second Sis. We were like a couple of young oxen, not fully grown but already aware we'd been born to be beasts of burden. Keeping our heads down and exerting our strength was all we could do, all we ought to do.

It was dusk and we had exhausted our energy, but there were still kilometers and kilometers to go. Farm fields and wilderness stretched on either side of the road, full of strange sounds and rustling. Past the fields was a hill, and darkness came rolling down to turn the world inky black. Second Sis produced a flatbread out of nowhere, broke off a small piece for herself, and gave me the rest. I didn't refuse but quickly demolished that two-thirds of a flatbread. Having eaten more, it was up to me to take the shafts. I understood more clearly now that we weren't just fetching coal to stoke cooking fires over the Spring Festival, but also to demonstrate to our neighbors that our family was doing well, that we could burn coal and not firewood. Even more importantly, Second Sis and I could brag to our friends and classmates, "We hauled coal! We're more grown up than you, and stronger too!" The villagers would spread the word, "Those Yan kids are quite something. Imagine walking almost a hundred kilometers at their age."

Alas, we couldn't move another inch.

We passed the sign for Minggao village, which meant we were fifteen kilometers from home, but it might as well have been the 3,000 kilometers that lay between the North and South of China. The night was impenetrable as mud. Through the stillness on either side came countless cracks and crunches as the ice thickened. The road had only been paved the year before and still gleamed darkly. In this faint glow, I asked Second Sis, "Do you think Mom and Dad will come for us?"

She stared into the distance ahead of us and, without a word, took my place between the shafts.

"I know Dad has asthma, but maybe Mom will come?" I said after we'd walked a little farther. She didn't answer my question but said the other villagers must be reaching home by now, and if we kept going, we'd get there soon too. We walked on with perseverance. Pulled the cart with perseverance. Walked a little, rested a little. Whenever we stopped, the sweat on our bodies chilled and froze, forcing us to move again. Then we'd hit another hill, or sometimes just level ground, and find we couldn't move another step. Whenever a truck passed by, lights blazing, the long-haul drivers looked godlike to us, nobly hauling several tons with just a foot on the pedal. Whenever a horse- or oxcart passed by, I thought how much better it would be to be livestock, so strong that no matter how heavy your load, you could keep your head down and carry on.

Being human and having to exert yourself is really a terrible thing. But if a person didn't need to lift a finger, if they could stay home in bad weather and still have food to eat and clothes to wear, wouldn't they basically be a god? I didn't want to be human any longer; I thought I might as well be an ox or a horse. I simply couldn't move another inch. When Second Sis saw that I was truly spent, she sat with me by the side of the road, staring into space. At first, we rested a few minutes then got moving again. Then a little longer. Soon, we were resting for as long as we'd been on the move. Half an hour of hauling, half an hour of resting. The road ahead, our future, seemed to retreat before us, and the more we walked the farther away home felt. Still, we had to keep going. Up ahead was where our home was. Walking in the direction of home is essentially moving toward a miracle. How would any of us be alive, if not for miracles? And sure enough, as if the heavens had seen that our strength was gone, divine intervention arrived. We were by the side of the road, searching for ice in the ditch to moisten our parched throats, when we heard someone calling, "Sufen! Lianke!" A lantern appeared out of the gloom. "Let there be light," said God, and amid the murk of humanity, there was light.

The Lord said, "Let there be food." And grain sprouted on the barren land.

The Lord said, "Someone will come get you." And here was our big brother.

He heard our cries and came running toward us.

When he'd learned that we were hauling coal, he came from the county seat to find us. It was a good fifteen kilometers in all seasons between our home and the county seat—the route never changed. He finished work at eight and came right away on his bicycle. That's why he was only arriving now, but that was better than if he hadn't intercepted us. If we'd already made it home, he'd have come all this way for nothing.

Here he was. Everything was all right. Life was beautiful, our hearts were clear, and new hope had arrived, as it always does, in a despairing world. Second Sis and I felt that this world and this day were warm as a coal fire in winter. The relief was like the electric fans and air-conditioning that city folk have whirring away in the summer.

Big Bro hooked his lantern to a shaft and told us to perch on the cart. What else could he do? He was our big brother. We sat on the front board, and he pulled us with more strength than a horse or ox.

How wonderful life was!

Second Sis and I clung on tight for fear of falling. I had one hand on a shaft, and with the other I took hold of Second Sis's hand. She had calluses on her palm, but otherwise it was as soft and tender as she was. Big Bro and the cart left one village behind. Then another. Here was the wooden bridge leading to our village, and there was our mother waiting for us. We went down the main road to our home. Big Sis and our father were waiting at the front door. The kinship of blood relations was like flames in winter, like a breeze in summer. We were bound together: Father, Mother, Big Sis,

Big Bro, Second Sis. Thank the heavens I'd been born into this family, that I had such parents and siblings.

It snowed heavily that Spring Festival, but the blazing fire fueled by the coal we'd brought back generated so much heat that even our drafty house remained snug. The neighbors came by for New Year, and our coal burned away all the cold in our village, in the whole world.

Senior High

Allow me to quote a passage I wrote about Second Sister in *Three Brothers*:

> It was also that year, as I was being promoted from middle school to high school, that I once again found my fate determined by my test scores. During that period, because I was so absorbed in literature, I became somewhat confused about real life. My fate, like that of my parents, was to work the land, so I would have no choice but to head out at dawn and work till dusk. I didn't believe that if you were able to get into high school, it might be possible for you to stop working the land and instead become a city resident. Therefore I became reconciled to my situation, thinking there was no way for me to advance. I attended that year's exams the same way that I would go with my classmates to watch an opera performance. At the time, the regulations for advancement specified that all the students with an urban residency permit would be automatically promoted, while those with rural residency permits would be promoted based on their test scores, plus letters of recommendation from their school and their production team. If you considered only test scores, Second Sister's were significantly higher than mine, but

if you took recommendations into account, she would probably fall back behind me, meaning that I would likely be the only one from our family who would advance to high school.

It was around lunchtime that Father brought home the news. It was summer, and the cicada cries were resonating through the tree branches. Father sat in our courtyard, and after explaining to Second Sister and me that only one of us could advance to high school, he just sat there, gazing at us uncomfortably. After a hesitation, he added, "Both of you understand our family's situation, in that we have many mouths to feed, and we also have to care for your elder sister. We really need for one of you to stay behind to work the land and earn some work points."

When Father finished, Second Sister and I stood in front of him holding our rice bowls, neither of us saying a word. There was a pause, as time itself ground to a halt and seemed as if it would never start flowing again. Fate froze between us, as clear water becomes bright ice, and it was as though time had become a block of ice pressing down on our family's courtyard. We remained frozen like this for a long time, a long, long time, until finally Mother emerged from the kitchen with a bowl of rice and said, "Come eat! You can continue discussing this after you've eaten."

We each went to eat our food.

I can't remember whether Second Sister carried her bowl inside or took it somewhere else. As for me, I took my bowl of boiled sweet potato noodles and unrefined black rice and went to sit under a tree. There was no one else under that tree, and as I sat all alone, I found that I simply couldn't summon the energy to eat that bowl of food. It was at that moment—as I was facing a crucial crossroads in my life and confronting the question of whether or not I would continue in school—that an educated youth arrived in our village, sent down from the city. He wore a blue uniform and had his hair parted on one side. He was tall, and as he strolled over from the village street, he nodded to the people he knew. The villagers spoke to him in a respectful tone, and he nodded lazily in return.

Then he walked away.

As for me, I sat there for a long time after he left, gazing at his departing shadow, as though looking at a road leading into the distance. At that moment, I realized that I wanted to continue my studies. I wanted to go to high school. I wanted to seize from Second Sister the slot she was probably counting on. So, I quickly ate my food and returned home, where I saw that Second Sister had reemerged to get more rice from the kitchen.

We gazed at each other as though we were complete strangers.

That afternoon, I went down to the fields to work, but for some reason Second Sister didn't go.

That night, Second Sister wasn't home for dinner.

After dinner, Second Sister still hadn't returned home.

I asked Mother, "Where is Second Sister?"

Mother replied, "She went to see her classmate."

I shifted questions of fate to the back of my mind, as though temporarily covering a wound with a piece of medicinal plaster. I went to sleep. The moon set, and the stars faded, and in the dim night light outside the window there was half-translucent fog and the sound of crickets. Eventually, in the middle of the night—just as I was about to fall asleep, or perhaps after I had already fallen asleep—I was suddenly aware of the sound of our front door opening. I heard Second Sister's soft footsteps out in the courtyard; they grew heavy as they approached my bedroom door. After a pause, Second Sister pushed open the door and approached my bed.

I sat up.

Second Sister said, "You haven't gone to sleep?"

I grunted in response.

Second Sister said, "Lianke, as for high school, your sister has decided she won't go. You should go."

Upon saying this, Second Sister gazed at me in the moonlight. I don't know whether she could see my expression, but I could vaguely make out her bleak smile. As she turned to leave, she said, "You should study well. Your sister is a girl, so she should stay home to work the land."

After that, there was a long wait for high school to begin. The day before school started, Second Sister bought me a fountain pen, and as she was giving it to me, she had tears in her eyes. Nevertheless, she forced a smile and said, "Study well. You need to make good on your sister's slot as well as your own."[1]

And so I enrolled in Song County Fourth High School, in the town where the philosophers Cheng Hao and Cheng Yi were born a thousand years ago. Even though I ended up only studying for another year before I had to drop out and look for work, that year of high school was a sacrifice my sister had made for me, pulverizing her own destiny and using it to build a road for my life. Without this road, without this extra year of education, I wouldn't have been able to pretend I'd finished high school and gotten into the army.

If I hadn't joined the army, my writing and my fate would have gone in a completely different direction, and I would be in a different place now.

Second Sis Gets Married

I went to school. I quit school and started work. I joined the army and left home.

I'd never thought about how time flows through a person's life like a river on a windy day. Is the wind moving the water, or does the rushing water give rise to the wind? After three years in the army, I was allowed a family visit, so I applied for leave to come home.

Home still looked like home. The toon tree by our front gate was the same size, and its few remaining withered leaves were raised to the sky, the same as always. The same number of leaves as when I left, every one of them in the same position, the precise shape I remembered.

Our roof had as many tiles as it had three years ago.

Our courtyard was still paved with the same red-veined stone slabs Second Sis and I had hauled from the Yi River in the eastern hills. Time had planted its feet here, or sat or lay down; at any rate it hadn't moved, even if people had insisted on ripping one page after another from the calendar to prove it was flowing on. I arrived home one evening in early winter, by which time the weary sun had settled down around the western hills. Because I was back, my mother was bustling around the kitchen making dinner in her usual flustered state, while my father was coughing away in his usual flustered state, stoking the fire in the breaks between hacking fits. Listening to him wheezing away, I realized what *had* changed at home, though it was hidden deep: My father's illness had gotten much worse. He was even sallower than before. The slightest wisp of cold air or speck of dust could set him coughing again, and he found it hard to stop. Now in a flustered state myself, I thumped him on the back, then I took the tongs from his hands and began adding wood to the fire and blowing on it. Idly, I asked, "Where's Second Sis?"

"She got married."

My father's voice was small but firm, as if he were merely saying she was still at work. I froze for a moment, watching the flickering flames, my tongs still among them. Everything was very quiet. The soft crackle of the fire was like the froth on the seashore being smothered by the next wave. I watched my father's face as, with a look of faint exasperation and unease, he said she'd been married for almost half a year to a reliable man from a well-off family in our village. Now her life would be stable. They hadn't told me because I wouldn't have been able to come to the wedding anyway. They thought it was better I didn't know, so I could focus on my work.

Once more I thought of the line: *That's how life is; you're cramped in on all sides, yet it keeps turning like a waterwheel.*

It was only me and my parents at dinner, the three of us huddled around the fire with our bowls. The world felt as vast and empty as it had when there was no one in it but a couple who'd recently moved out of the Garden of Eden, and their children. I recall none of us speaking, but I also have a recollection of saying a lot to each other. After the meal, Second Sis and her husband came by. Big Sis and her husband came too. The whole family sat around the fire. I said nothing, yet it felt as if a lot had been said. The night deepened, and the already silent house somehow began to accumulate layers of awkwardness. I knew this strangeness came from my brothers-in-law, strangers who hadn't yet been accepted by us. Not because of who they were, whether they were rich or poor, intelligent or stupid, garrulous or quiet, but simply because they had taken away Big Sis and Second Sis. I couldn't understand why my parents had worked so hard to raise these women for over twenty years, only to let them get taken away like that. On that night, I looked at my sisters and their husbands from the depths of resentment and jealously, simmering in silent resentment. I barely spoke a word all evening. Lateness encroached. Big Sis and her husband rose to leave, and so did Second Sis and her husband. I walked out with them, and in the courtyard Second Sis turned and said to me, "You're not that young anymore, you should be looking for a mate. You don't want to leave Mom and Dad all alone at home, do you?"

Again I thought: *That's how life is, you're cramped in on all sides, yet it keeps turning like a waterwheel.* That's life!

Interlude 3

For some reason, I feel like I ought to have an interlude here.

My sisters getting married made me think of the role of revolution and calculation at one particular moment in the history of rural marriage. During that era, revolution provided the structure for marriage, and under the shroud of revolution, the calculations and considerations of marriage were what allowed it to rupture and break free of this framework. Prior to 1949, Big Sis's husband's father joined the army to survive, and ended up fighting for the Kuomintang so he could fill his belly. During the successive post-1949 revolutionary movements, he was attacked and paraded through the streets, and his family was doomed to a tragic, uncertain fate. The same went for his son's marriage prospects. It didn't matter how handsome or accomplished the boy was, revolutionary society shunned him like a weed by the side of the road, a thorny vine hanging off a cliff. Then in 1978, the political situation changed and "class" was once again determined by economics, which released his family from their bind. Now that his background was no longer problematic, he was free to marry my sister.

Second Sis married into a family less marked by class and politics, but pragmatic considerations were still a key part of her calculus. She chose her husband not just because he was reliable and sincere but also because he was from our village, so they knew everything about each other's families, with all the judgment, calculation, and reckoning that implied. For instance, my brother-in-law was an only son. He had older and younger sisters, but they would eventually marry out of the family, which meant there would be no disputes over inheritance or property. Also, he "had a position," which came with proper wages. He worked at the county's machine factory. Having lived a life of poverty, my father had said his son-in-law was well-off, meaning that he had a reliable means of making a living. And he chose Second Sis for similar considerations (calculations): the relative wealth and stability of our family, and our long-standing good reputation in the village. And so, Second Sis married Second Brother-in-Law. It seems that their considerations (calculations) were a good metric for a village marriage, but with the benefit of hindsight, these considerations point more to the fundamental nature of marriage as a means of getting by, as well as a form of pushback against the revolution-shrouded institution of marriage. In any case, my sisters got married of their own free will. In the course of their marriage, though, for all that they were able to choose their mates, social pressure placed many nonnegotiable conditions on them. Amid this jumble, their lives and marriage might have come under the banner of freedom but were still restricted by social conditions and the dominant powers in the village.

There is one element of Chinese village marriages that are the same anywhere else in the world: Love is an add-on that often fades or vanishes from a marriage thanks to compulsion, power, or reason, leaving one of many other social constructs to take its place. That's how it was with both my sisters' marriages and lives, as well as for virtually all the women in the village going a century back. At the end of the day, no matter who you are or what kind of marriage or family you have, this remains true: You can enter a marriage or family through a number of wide entrances, but you'll only be able to exit through a single narrow door.

Sister-in-Law

It's time to talk about my sister-in-law.

She's a medical worker in the county seat. I don't know how she and my brother met. One year, I came home for a visit, and there she was, presenting me with a sweater she'd knitted for me. My brother said, "This is your sister-in-law." I froze, and all I could say was: "Hello." How could this be my sister-in-law? I don't know what I'd expected my brother's wife to look like, but she wasn't right for the role. She seemed perfectly respectable, well-spoken, and polite, but still I thought, *How could this be my sister-in-law? How is she a part of our family?* Our surname is Yan but hers is Cui. How could a family come from different origins? My sisters getting married made me feel the household had collapsed, but my sister-in-law's arrival wasn't doing anything to fill the sinkhole they'd left. It didn't take long, though, for me to feel she *was* my sister-in-law, and that she was exactly what had been missing from our family.

Family secrets are a doorway for the narrator. Enter this door and you'll see my parents' vendetta against Third Uncle, who was actually my father's cousin—their fathers were brothers, which meant his children were my second cousins. Still, he was a close blood relation. Despite this closeness, my parents spent years yelling, raging, sobbing, and accumulating resentment against Third Uncle and Third Aunt-in-Law, because of the "living wall" between our courtyards. When building his house, Third Uncle's floor plans shifted this shared wall toward us by half its width. Looking with today's eyes at our village's dead walls, private walls, or living walls, when you saw two families with neighboring fields coming to blows or even resorting to bloodshed because one of them had plowed an extra row or taken a shovelful of the other's land, it felt like two starving men arguing over which of them had a thicker waist or a little more height. Because of the tiny strip of land beneath the wall, Father and Third Uncle feuded year after year, steadily refusing to make peace. Third Uncle was unable to have a conversation without raising his voice. Raising his voice led to a fight. Fighting made him reach for a shovel or ax. As a result, every one of their disputes ended with my parents crashing down onto their bed, sighing and weeping. As for their four kids, we could only stand by with our heads down, not daring to say a word.

One summer, when I was in my teens, our families got into yet another squabble about the moving of the wall, and whether it was living or dead. Third Uncle held a gleaming round-headed shovel and stood by our front door, roaring, "Come out, any of you, and I'll chop off your head! Two come out, a pair of heads will roll!" At his instigation, Third Aunt-in-Law was there too, cursing so vehemently that her words were hard to absorb and impossible to repeat. A dozen villagers crowded round to watch, then a few dozen, and soon more than a hundred. Amid this clamor, my father felt compelled to have his say. If he didn't respond, he'd have no dignity left. He told us, "I'm going out so your third uncle can hack me to death in the street. Remember how I died." He stood up calmly from his stool, got dressed, fastened his buttons, and strolled out. We tried to pull him back, but he yelled in the direction of Third Uncle and Aunt-in-Law, "My kids are too young to die. If you *must* kill someone today, you can chop my head off, but let my wife and children live."

Third Uncle froze.

Third Aunt-in-Law stopped swearing and also froze.

The summer afternoon heat was like boiling water. The gawkers stared at my father, faces flustered, pale and sweaty. Maybe Third Uncle hadn't expected him to come within shovel range, or else he'd been waiting for this moment to bring the shovel down on his head. My mother charged out too and tried to drag my father back in. He pushed her off and said, "Make sure you bring up our children properly when I'm dead." And then he walked out.

My siblings and I stood in the courtyard, agape. We hurried after our father and watched him striding toward Third Uncle and the crowd. None of us grabbed his leg to hold him back, nor did we reach for a shovel, ax, or cleaver so we'd be armed and ready to fight Third Uncle. We just stared, waiting for whatever would happen next to play out. Weakness and terror had us in their grip, just as a mutating tumor can control a person's life.

Step by step, our father approached Third Uncle.

The onlookers were so silent that I could hear them breathing, like the wind that rushed past the village walls. Father drew closer. Third Uncle, seemingly incapable of retreat, held up his shovel and screamed, "You think I don't dare?" He raised the blade over his head and lunged. The entire crowd shrieked, "Aah!" Someone leaped forward to pull him back.

Now both sides were in battle formation. Father and Third Uncle were held five or six paces apart. Father stopped and glared at Third Uncle, who stayed rooted to the ground with his shovel in the air. Stalemate. Eventually, the standoff broke up when people wouldn't stop yelling, "You're cousins! You're cousins!" It still took Third Uncle quite a while to shout, "Seeing as we're cousins, I'll put away my shovel for today."

He lowered his arm, turned around, and went back home with his shovel.

The incident ended with the villagers hauling my father back inside, and my mother glaring at the four of us. "Your father spent all these years raising you, and you just stand there and let him get hacked to death?" In her voice we heard gentle disapproval and regret at having raised us at all. Her voice was raspy and sharp, and her eyes gleamed coldly and pointedly. To this day I can recall her reproachful eyes and tone, and it sends a shiver through me. At that moment, I had no idea what to say in response, but I lacked the courage to face Third Uncle when he had the shovel held above him like a blade.

I was quite a feeble, timid person in youth and middle age, and I still am today. Fear wraps around me like a snake. Around my pen, my limbs, my destiny. If someone were to ask me what torments me more than anything in life, I'd answer without hesitation, "Cowardice!"

Cowardice shaped my fate and my writing, and also determined my siblings' lives and marriages, the families they formed and the lives they've led.

After Third Uncle raised a shovel to Father and Father offered himself up to be hacked apart, the blood ties between our households ruptured. We still appeared united, but we began drifting apart, month after month, year after year, until several years later when we moved out of that house. We'd thought this was a great way to resolve this territorial dispute, but we hadn't anticipated that seeing our house empty, Third Uncle would decide to tear down the wall and further encroach on our property. My father was no longer with us, I was still in the army, my brother was living in the county seat, and my sisters were married. That left no one around to risk life and limb to put a stop to this, as my father had. And even if we'd had the courage and strength to confront Third Uncle and Aunt-in-Law, none of us could have talked sense into them. Mother called my brother to ask what she should do, but after an agonizing discussion, they didn't come up with any ideas. It was my sister-in-law who, after eavesdropping on the call, hurried back to our hometown. She got off the bus and didn't even stop by our home but made a beeline for Third Uncle's house, where she found him in the process of laying a foundation, just as he had been when my father confronted him all those years ago. She stood in his yard, completely unflustered, and asked him why he was doing this. Why was it important to take up that little extra bit of land? What was the point, she asked, giving himself just a chopstick's width more? Was he after more parking space? Did he want to turn his courtyard into Tiananmen Square? Was he planning to hold large gatherings and public assemblies? Also, he should know that she'd recently married into the Yan family, which made her one of us, and if Third Uncle wanted a fight, he should feel free to hack her to death. Or if he preferred to sue, she was prepared to quit her job and see him and Third Aunt-in-Law in court. She walked toward him as she spoke. It was her first visit as his niece-in-law, she said, how terribly rude to have come empty-handed, she really ought to have brought some nourishing foods from the county seat and presented them to Third Uncle where he was sitting on the ground, courteously and respectfully.

"Third Uncle, Third Aunt-in-Law," said my sister-in-law. "Is it worth it, at your age? You've spent your lives squabbling and losing your tempers over a meager inch of land. Can you take an inch of land to the grave? Will it let you live another decade? Do you think you'll live as long as the land? If you could take it with you, if it meant you'd live another hundred years, then of course I wouldn't begrudge you this sliver of land. I'd let you have the whole courtyard, if it were up to me. But if there's no point, please stop laying that foundation, and come back to the county seat with me. I'll take you to the hospital there for a full checkup, and they'll treat whatever's wrong with you so you can keep living in good health. That's the most important thing for old people like you. Why fuss over an inch of land?"

That solved the whole problem.

Third Uncle obediently stopped his campaign of expansion and never again said a word about the issue that had dominated his life: whether this was a living or dead wall. After my sister-in-law's barnstorming speech, Third Uncle, Third Aunt-in-Law, and my mother were able to mend their relationship.

I adore my sister-in-law.

This incident made clear that my sister-in-law is the most upright and dignified person in our clan. She is also the backbone of the household, taking on a thousand tasks just as my parents did. The sinkhole left by the departure of my sisters was filled by her and my wife; new blood ties and affection turned the depression into a hill. At a much later point, I was talking to my brother's daughter, Fangfang, and she said, "My ma is great in every way, except she talks too much. She makes noise all day long. All the streets and alleyways in the whole city couldn't contain her voice and all her opinions."

3
The Aunts

Eldest Aunt

I don't know my eldest aunt's name, and I never thought of asking my parents. At some point in the distant past, I became aware that she was my father's big sister, and she'd married into a village less than five kilometers away called Zhaigou, or Stockade Valley. One year, my siblings and I went to visit, and we found it didn't take us long to get there. The so-called "valley" was just a dip, with the houses and river following the slope of the hills. Eldest Aunt's home was by the village entrance and consisted of three sturdy thatched buildings, a spick-and-span low-roofed kitchen of compressed earth, and a courtyard that remained spotless because its dirt had been mixed with sand and compacted. Inside they had pictures of a bodhisattva and Chairman Mao on the wall, an incense burner, ancestral tablets, and other miscellaneous objects on a long table.

All the houses in this village seemed to have main rooms laid out in this manner, as systematic as my eldest aunt being called "Eldest Aunt," and my third aunt "Third Aunt." There was a question about Eldest Aunt that I pondered for decades without arriving at an answer; I didn't ask anyone about it either. She was extremely attractive, with a tall, willowy figure and bound feet, a square, ruddy face and long hair that she always kept in a bun. Her pale face, pink cheeks, and large eyes that always held the hint of a smile gave her the wise, benevolent appearance of a bodhisattva.

In fact, I found the bodhisattva less beautiful than my aunt.

Her husband, though, was leagues behind her. He wasn't too short, but his skin was very coarse, his face was the color of mud, and his voice boomed like a meteor shower. And also ... okay, I'll just say it: He was hard of hearing in both ears, which made every conversation with him sound like we were arguing.

How could Eldest Aunt have given herself to him? A poor, ugly, shouty man who ... well, he had a good personality, he was strong and loved to work, and he was the best ox handler in all of Zhaigou. He treated those oxen as tenderly as if they were his own children. If he ever saw anyone swat an ox for no reason, he'd yell at them that oxen are living things too, that they have souls, they weren't just put on earth to pull our plows and carts. Their lives are already hard enough; why would you hit them?

Was that why Eldest Aunt married him?

That hardly seemed worth it to me.

Anyway, there I was, having stumbled my way into my teens, when I found out that Eldest Aunt's only daughter was adopted. This added to the mystery of Eldest Uncle-in-Law. I guessed this meant one of them had some kind of reproductive issue—but which one? Deductive reasoning led me to Eldest Aunt. Maybe *that's* why she had to marry this man. And his poverty, ugliness, and disability gave him no choice but to accept her. But how did she learn she couldn't have kids? Had she been married before? Wouldn't my parents and uncles have mentioned that? My youngest aunt made a love match and chose a slender, handsome, well-educated man who spirited her away to the mountains dozens of kilometers away, where the flat land in front of their house got treated by the other villagers like a town square, and so those of us who actually lived in a town—including my family—frequently made fun of her for suffering this consequence of her romance. Youngest Aunt's marriage served as a cautionary tale for our entire village, which didn't seem able to stop talking about it. If Eldest Aunt had indeed been married before, there's no way these gossips would have been discreet about it. Maybe not a marriage, then, but some premarital indiscretion? My father and uncles would certainly have kept mum about anything that sordid, like a sheepskin-bound tome my mother and aunts were allowed to read when they married into the Yan family, a secret to be passed down to future generations like an heirloom.

Yet there was not a hint of anything like that.

Eldest Aunt's life was complete, like a tarpaulin that wind or rain couldn't penetrate. She and her husband never argued or got unhappy with each other. Eldest Uncle-in-Law didn't seem to resent her in any way. When he was plowing, she'd climb the hill with his lunch pail, which saved him the trip back so he could have a nap in the field. When he was ferrying villagers in his oxcart to our town for market day or to a gathering farther afield, she'd go to the village gate after dusk and wait there with a lantern to welcome him home. The oxcart would arrive full of villagers laden with purchases from town, and Eldest Uncle-in-Law would invariably get a bundle of superior incense sticks for Eldest Aunt. She burned these as an offering to the bodhisattva; they let off white smoke and a pure fragrance, with an ash column that stood tall and proud, never crumbling.

Their love was a paragon for our entire clan. My parents, aunts, and uncles kept urging, "I hope you all live your lives like your eldest aunt and uncle." But the waterwheel of time kept turning, and not a single person in my generation, not my siblings or cousins or over a hundred people across dozens of households, managed to find an existence as serene as Eldest Aunt and her husband, free of quarrels, of all the incomprehension and suspicion that men and women have for each other buried beneath mundane, undemonstrative love.

Interlude 4

It's now been over a decade since Eldest Aunt left us, and Eldest Uncle-in-Law has been dead for almost twenty years. As I sit here writing this memoir, what comes to mind isn't the minutiae of their lives or their long and loving relationship, but the confusion I felt about Eldest Aunt's existence and home life as a teen. Why did she marry Eldest Uncle-in-Law? Did her half-bound feet trip her up on the way to freedom? When the winds of revolution blew across the Central Plains, did they sweep her off those tiny feet? Or was it that my grandparents, unable to stand her cries of agony when they crushed her feet, gave in to their tender feelings and loosened her bindings? Most importantly, did she have a previous marriage, and if not, how did such a beauty give herself to a man whose likeness, personality, and disposition might as well have been sculpted from mud? How could they have formed this enduring love buried beneath their ordinary lives, like a warm and silent river? I boldly imagined the romantic adventures she might have had in the past, followed by the tragedy that forced her to accept his proposal and humble herself before the bodhisattva every day. Did that mean my lowly uncle was a noble part of China's recent history, playing a crucial role in the struggle for women's freedom and equality in the countryside?

I didn't have a single clue.

I had no more idea about Eldest Aunt's life than I could have told you how many hairs I had on my head.

So many social and feminist issues could have taken root and flourished in her life: the liberation of married women, women in general, humanity; the freedom to choose our own life partners; the choice to have or not have children; whether to raise children in a village; their education and living environment; the intersections and contradictions of these issues. Sadly, my eldest aunt and uncle-in-law brought all of these into the next world with them.

Of all the relatives in my parents' generation, only my mother and youngest aunt are still alive. If I wanted *The Women* to be a record of rural feminist thought and history, I'd be rushing off to interview them, camera and recording device in hand.

Alas, I have no such aspiration. I'm just writing a book of essays.

Second Aunt, Third Aunt, Cousin

My second aunt got married and moved to Tengwanggou, a village less than ten kilometers west of ours. She was dead by the time I learned she was in this distant place, apparently from a rare illness. As a result, she's always been a vague, tragic figure to me. As a young man, whenever I passed that remote village, I'd think, "My second aunt got married and moved here. My second aunt left this world long ago." Her marriage, death, and absence would haunt my footsteps and seep up through my shoes and socks.

Third Aunt married halfway up Jiugao Mountain to the east of us. Li Bai once climbed the peak above her village and wrote two poems there, one of which—"Jiugao Crane Cry"—is still memorized and recited in my hometown today. I wrote about Third Aunt and her family in *A Child of Tianhu*, setting down every detail until I had nothing left to say, like when you've emptied out a bucket but still have to carry it around. Though I did leave out one thing, and I'm going to make up for that now. Speaking of this feels like picking up a tear that has frozen solid, diamond-like.

Third Aunt had a son and a daughter, my cousins. All of a sudden, I realized my female cousin had grown up. Just as abruptly, she got married. One summer's day when I was in middle school, I returned home at lunchtime and found Third Aunt sobbing as she told her little brother, my father, that her daughter was getting divorced after less than a year of marriage. "He doesn't want her anymore," she wept. "She's always slept a lot—I could never get her to wake up." This was fine when she was living at home, but when her husband's family couldn't rouse her in the morning, they decided she was a lazy good-for-nothing.

The house and courtyard looked the same, the summer was still scorching, yet the atmosphere felt completely different. Third Aunt and my parents were usually warm and friendly, but now everything felt heavy and sad, like we were wading through mud. None of us could imagine getting divorced because of drowsiness. Then again, during the summer wheat harvest, when everyone was so busy that they didn't even have time to breathe, how could you refuse to wake up? They'd shake her and place her scythe next to the bed, but she'd say, "I'll be there in a minute," then roll over and go right back to sleep.

Her husband and his parents would spend half the day harvesting, then come back and find her still in bed.

Hence, divorce.

My cousin knelt down and pleaded for another chance, but there was no saving this marriage. Third Aunt cried so hard, her face was completely bloodless. This was so humiliating that no one could ever find out. "Imagine getting divorced for sleeping too much! How could I explain that to anyone? They'd never understand!" After sneaking home with her possessions, my cousin kept saying she wanted to kill herself, which is why Third Aunt hurried home once she'd told my father everything, not even staying for lunch.

Father told me to go with her.

I walked my aunt to the wooden bridge over the Yi River, outside our village. As I watched her disappear into the murky days ahead, it felt as if she were walking deep into the swamp of fate, seeking her own death.

My cousin eventually got remarried to a much older, previously married man who lived on the other side of the mountains. We heard his wife had died suddenly, leaving him with two young children and no one to take care of them. My cousin was willing to be a stepmother. No one knew about her second marriage, just as no one knew about her divorce. Before setting off, she told Third Aunt and Third Uncle-in-Law that she wouldn't be coming back home if she could help it, nor would she return to Tianhu to see her uncles. Her life was so embarrassing, she didn't want to have to explain it to anyone.

Many years later, my spine and back were giving me trouble, so I went to Xi'an for massage and acupuncture. I told this story to the acupuncturist, who smiled and said, "Sleeping too much is an illness of the central nervous system. Tell her to come see me. Two days of acupuncture, and she'll sleep and get up like a normal person." I went home with the happy news, but no one—not my mother, sisters, sister-in-law, or even my uncle's kids—knew where she was, and they hadn't been in touch with her for more than a decade. This was after my father, Third Aunt, and her husband had passed away. A whole generation was gone, like a felled swath of forest. There was no way to track down my cousin—the road leading to her no longer existed. We had no idea how she was doing, or if her condition was any better.

A few days later, I regretfully went back to my unit. Every time I thought of Third Aunt, I also thought of my cousin, as if it were my cousin who'd stirred up these memories. In the end, our moral sense can't stand up to time, destiny, and separation. Eventually, my cousin slipped from my memory. I can't remember what Eldest Aunt or Third Aunt looked like, and now the cruelty of the mind has wiped away my cousin too.

Interlude 5

If it isn't too contrived, I'd like to reach into this thicket of female relatives, my aunts and cousin, and draw a conclusion: Whether in the city or countryside, or any family in the grip of patriarchal society, women were forgotten very quickly. On the road between marriage and the grave, no records existed for daughters (or women). Women who entered their graves as daughters-in-law only made it onto the final scroll of the annals on the coattails of a man. Second Aunt's marriage and early death prove that memory leaves, never to return. All traces of her life vanished when she got married, which wiped her from the Yan family's recollections. No one mentioned her, no one asked about her, not even her brothers, my uncles and father. Without meaning to, they allowed her to be erased.

When Eldest Aunt and Third Aunt died, they weren't buried in our family tomb, but in their husbands' family plots. An exchange of memory: They went away, and in return we got my mother and my uncles' wives, who in turn had to cut the thread to their birth families and put down roots in ours. That's how we were so easily and heartlessly able to forget my cousin, as if it didn't matter to us if she lived or died. I include myself in this. As the saying goes, "A married daughter is like water you've poured away." This is the most callous attitude China takes toward women, death by a gentle knife. Like when my father's sisters got married and moved away, and their daughters subsequently got married, splashing the water even farther from us. Like a train splitting and half the carriages going down a different track, then splitting again onto yet another branch, for better or worse. We are only mindful of ourselves and what's right in front of us, so no one gave a single thought to their lives or destinies. It made perfect sense to scrub them from our minds, a sort of premature death. My cousin's divorce and remarriage no longer had anything to do with us.

No one felt guilty about forgetting my cousin. No one thought of moral memory as actual memory. Even now, writing this book, how much do I really remember? Other than her sleeping too much since she was a child, whether it was a quirk or an illness, everything else about her has been pushed by men into an abyss of ignorance. Our neglect and erasure of her mirrors the way we go to my parents' and grandparents' graves every Tomb-Sweeping Day to pay our respects, mourn and remember them, yet we've never once visited my aunts' burial sites.

Because they were women—village women. If village society is an ancient, overgrown wilderness, the villagers are the ones who tamed it, yet when these pioneers depart, the tombstones in the fields have the men's names, not the women's. As if there were never any women pouring their sweat, tears, and blood into this soil.

Memory wipes clean the slate when women get married, but no one thinks of memory as a murderer. No one is responsible for these killings, just as no one believes that women ought not to get married.

Youngest Aunt

My youngest aunt got married and moved very far away.

Back when horse- and oxcarts were the main forms of transport, each time a car or bus rumbled past our village, that was as exciting as drums and cymbals on a festive day. From my description, you're probably imagining some primeval era, perhaps back when Pangu separated the heavens and earth, and time itself still bore the marks and mossy growths of that distant age. Roads hadn't appeared beneath our feet. Lakes hadn't been carved from the land. Oceans did not yet know where their shores were. The plains and forests were still jumbled together. But no, I'm not looking that far back. Rather, this was a mere few decades ago, when your fathers were growing their first beards and your mothers were putting together their meager trousseaus without yet knowing where they were being married off to.

At the time, though, Youngest Aunt *did* know where she was going.

Love called to her like the sun summoning a sunflower. Youngest Uncle-in-Law was an accountant at the grain station in town. Not only was he literate and able to read a newspaper, he knew his way around an abacus. This was the 1950s, when education was not just a ray of divine light falling from the heavens; it was also a hefty weight on the scale of romance. After considering every possible factor, Youngest Aunt didn't find any reason not to love this man. Sure, he came from a village so remote it might as well be in Africa; even if you went by the widest, flattest road available, the oxen pulling your cart would be panting heavily all the way. That's where she decided she was going. The power of love is a locomotive engine pulling a lightweight carriage with rubber wheels. They chose each other freely, out of love, like lanterns sending out searching beams. My grandparents and other villagers opposed this match, but one morning she was gone, along with her clothes and a bundle of possessions.

She had flown off in the direction of love.

What was the name of her new village? No one knew.

The man she was marrying—what was his family like? No one knew.

How far was this place from the prosperous village known as Tianhu? There was no answer that could fill in these blanks, only the unspoken ones: freedom and love. Thinking back, my youngest aunt and her husband were the first proponent of free love in our village on the Central Plains. These days, we all walk down the path of liberation, tenderness, and romance, a path they forged for us through thorny undergrowth, marked with their footprints and tears. Lu Xun said, "When many people walk this way, a road will appear"; he meant people like Youngest Aunt and Uncle-in-Law, those right at the forefront.

My father described his first visit to her: "It was as far away as the edge of the sky. I thought my ankles were going to snap clean in two."

My eldest uncle: "They have great wild grass over there. I cut a few scythe loads, to thatch our roof with."

My mother summed things up neatly and decisively, with an air of compressed philosophy: "It's all down to fate. Fate arranges the life of a man as if he's its own son. But for a woman's life, it's as if she's only its stepdaughter."

When I was finally able to visit Youngest Aunt's home, there was a road climbing up the mountain range, winding like a snake. I waited an hour for the bus, then stood on the crowded bus for two and a half hours. That stressful journey was followed by half a day's walk. I'd set off at daybreak, and the sun was setting over the mountains when I finally reached Liujiajian, a village of twenty-some households situated on either side of a mountain road, mostly on the gentler slope, but a handful farther off, virtually hanging over a cliff. Youngest Aunt was in one of those cliff-top houses. Three well-constructed thatched buildings, two slightly lower side chambers, a kitchen, a mill room, and in the yard a pigsty, cow pen, and chicken coop, plus a pile of firewood and fallen branches as tall as the shed. By the front gate were a few dozen square meters of flatland, which everyone called a square, and if you took a step forward you'd be at the edge of a seemingly bottomless ravine. It was April and the warmth of spring had belatedly arrived, which filled the hills with magnificent red peonies and glittering yellow winter jasmine.

Had Youngest Aunt moved here for this gorgeous landscape?

Who knows.

Did she regret getting married? Did she complain about her fate?

You'd have to ask her yourself!

Yes, Youngest Aunt ought to answer these questions herself. Never in my hearing did my father or uncles ponder whether she regretted eloping. When my mother asked her this question in front of us kids, she answered with certainty, "What's there to regret? My life is amazing! I don't need to worry about anything. I have plenty of food and clothes." It didn't matter who asked her; that's all she would say, beaming away.

The sixties and seventies were filled with fires of revolution that all but burned away human desire. Communism was too perfect as a spiritual ideal, making the gut desire for material things feel as meaningless as a wish for fresh air. I can't remember how Youngest Aunt and the others survived the years of the great famine, but I do recall my mother telling me that Youngest Aunt and her husband would walk a long way to come visit, bringing a sack of wheat bran to use as pig feed, after which she'd tell her brothers, "I was right to marry him. No one has starved to death where we are." In the sixties, when food was scarce again, anyone who ate wheat noodles or rice outside of Spring Festival would feel guilt-ridden, like a thief. Deep in the mountains where my aunt was, the revolutionary drumbeat wasn't as ear-splitting, and people had time and energy to plant staple foods, which meant they could sometimes eat pillowy steamed buns and oil-tossed noodles even when it wasn't a holiday.

During that time, my favorite place to visit on vacation was Youngest Aunt's home. You could catch crabs in the creek there, and during the hay harvest you could climb trees to steal bird's nests. Back at the house, Youngest Aunt would make me a bowl of garlicky wheat noodles. Or dough fritters fried golden and crisp in cottonseed oil, a snack fit for an emperor. At the end of the summer, they would send me back home with a sack of refined wheat flour, fresh from the mill, for my father.

After my father got ill, every time Youngest Aunt came back for a visit, she invariably brought refined flour and noodles made from finely ground mung beans.

On one of these visits, she sat by her big brother's bedside and they talked late into the night. All of a sudden, my father told my mother to shut the front door. He sank into thought for a while, looked all around, and said to my youngest aunt, "The Revolution's been harsh, food is running short, and everyone's afraid of starving through another of 'those three years.'" (He meant the Great Leap Forward.) In order to stave off the coming famine, he urged my aunt to start stockpiling grain. She smiled mysteriously and told my father not to worry; she might live in the remote mountains, but she certainly hadn't lost her wits. Her clan remembered well how people had starved to death during "those three years," and to make sure it didn't happen again, they'd been rationing grain and storing the surplus in giant vats, which they'd buried on their property, insulated with lime.

My parents stared at Youngest Aunt in shocked delight, then smiles of relief spread across their faces. A moment like God separating day from night. Lamps powered by the electric current from Luoyang city shone on their faces; they looked like holy worshippers of grain, as if the messiah of grain had passed his sacred hands over their heads, and their features glowed with contentment and bliss. They knew the great flood of hunger was coming, but they had no fear, thanks to the Noah's ark of stockpiled grain.

They fell silent, still smiling. After an eternity, my father said Youngest Aunt's name, "Cui." Another moment of silence. Then, with all the wisdom of an elder brother, "You were right to elope. Your life is better than your sisters'"—my eldest, second, and third aunts.

I glimpsed tears in my youngest aunt's eyes. Her smile had never been so radiant. The smile of a god on a mortal's face.

The night continued to deepen, and our days were filled with lyrical love.

Interlude 6

My youngest aunt is now in her eighties. For over sixty years, life, love, and happenstance bound her existence to this clifftop village, where she raised livestock and planted crops, ran a household and faced down days of labor in those fields and valleys. When she looks back over her life, whether on her all-encompassing love or on the silent isolation that followed her grand passion, I don't know whether she feels able to accept without complaint all that was heaped upon her. All I can say is we've never heard her utter a single word of resentment or regret against her fate, just as my eldest aunt seldom said anything against her husband. Youngest Aunt's four daughters married into villages far away, while her two sons took a path at the dawn of their youth that led them away from these hills to a city, or farther afield to Kashgar in Xinjiang. Youngest Aunt currently lives alone on the cliff top. Her husband left this world twenty years ago. They raised six descendants, and my aunt handled their marriages, apart from that of their eldest daughter, Aixiang. Interestingly, she didn't put any conditions on who they should marry, leaving them to make their own choices. She did lean on her sons to head for the cities, where there was more going on and it would be easier to earn money. If the daughters weren't able to marry into a city, she hoped they would at least end up somewhere closer to a main travel route, so it would be more convenient for them to get to the nearest market town.

I have no way of guessing at my youngest aunt's understanding or opinions about marriage, love, and women, those deceptively simple yet profound issues. She was a pioneer in my family for going flat out after the man she loved. As if to prove the choice she made of her own free will was the right one, she never said she wished she hadn't done it. In the many, many years that followed, she proved she'd chosen correctly, not because her relationship with my uncle was a beacon of sacred love, but simply because she had more food than she could ever eat.

China's history has never broken free of village life, nor has it ever risen sharply like skyscrapers in a growing city. My aunt was able to choose her husband because of history, but she also had to navigate a vast historical wound—famine and starvation, those utterly material conditions—to justify the rectitude and wisdom of what she did. By the same logic, authors can only write novels if they have food to fill their bellies, so it feels as if at mealtimes they're also placing dishes of spirituality and philosophy on the dining table. Youngest Aunt planted crops when others did, built a house when others did. When others left home to earn money, she encouraged her children to do the same in Guangzhou or Shenzhen. Time and the material world were an ocean around the island of my youngest aunt's mind and spirit.

The place where my aunt lives, still as remote as an African village, is now completely empty of young people. They haven't just gone to seek work; they've married and settled down in more prosperous places, trying to get closer to the towns and cities. Many of the elders followed their kids out of there. Now there are only a few households left, with maybe a couple of dozen people, waiting for the extinction of their village and generation. My brother, sisters, and mother have suggested many times that she could move back home, where her life would be more convenient and secure. She could move in with us and enjoy the comforts of town in her remaining years, but she always adamantly refuses. "I'm not going anywhere. I'm staying right here, in this village and in this house."

Juan Rulfo's short story "Luvina" tells of all the men and boys forsaking the gray mountain town of Luvina for work in the city, leaving women and the elderly behind. When someone asks the women why they didn't follow their menfolk, they answer as one, "But if we leave, who'll carry our dead? They live here and we can't leave them behind."[1] That's pretty much what Youngest Aunt said. I could even believe that this story, written in Mexico in the 1950s, was a piece of nonfiction set in a hilly region in the North of China. My youngest aunt continues to live in her village, where wild rabbits recently started running through her courtyard, and the howls of wolves can be heard nearby. I went there myself not long ago, hoping to bring her home to live with my mother, but she said without hesitation, "If I go, what's going to happen to your uncle-in-law?"

My uncle-in-law's name was Wang Fulai. As a teenager, he was already reading books and newspapers, and he could put any number into the twelve strings of his abacus, no matter how astronomical. He was the one who came up with my name, Lianke, a little gift he presented me with at my birth. His reasoning was, "There are many people in Soviet Russia called Lianke." ["Lianke" is common in the transliteration of Russian names, such as "Jiri Lianke" for "Kirilenko."]

4
The Aunts-in-Law

Eldest Aunt-in-Law

I don't know how my eldest aunt-in-law ended up married to my father's brother. I almost never heard my cousins talking about visiting her parents, not even at Spring Festival.

It was as if they were growing up without grandparents on their mother's side.

If that were the case, how tragic my aunt-in-law's life must be. Perhaps she had a childhood as dark as the water that the calligrapher Wang Xizhi washed his ink brushes in? What murk she must have sprung from. And yet, as far back as I can remember, she always had a smile on her face as she went around humming snatches of traditional opera or Henan village ditties, like an actor who'd been forced to leave the stage for some reason, and who now spent every waking moment singing to prove she was different from other villagers, other women, as if she were a princess who had to warble away in order to show how wonderful her marriage to the prince was.

Sometimes my eldest uncle would make fun of her to us and the other villagers, saying she even sang opera in her dreams. No one had any idea why she was so overjoyed the whole time, as if the hardship and bitterness of their lives didn't touch her. In *Three Brothers*, I described in detail how my uncle and his family suffered through that era of Chinese history, how their days were an undrinkable soup of chili, vinegar, goldthread, and gall. Two adults and eight children living through a winter without shoes or socks for the kids, so they had to tramp barefoot through the snow. Making a big pot of vegetable stew and remembering at the last minute to scatter in some noodles or corn, then going through every jar and tin only to find them all empty. Chinese households traditionally place the women in charge of everything indoors while men handle the outside world, but Eldest Aunt-in-Law didn't believe in this long-standing division of labor. When her children didn't have shoes, she'd stand at her front door and scream, "How am I meant to take care of so many kids?" When she had a pot on the stove and realized the cupboard was bare, she'd turn off the flame and head out with a large bowl or scoop, humming all the way, dropping in on us or another neighbor to borrow some flour or grain. Then she'd hum her way home to light the fire and cook yet another of their three meals a day.

Hardship seemed pleasurable to her.

She accepted and even welcomed it like the ocean receiving hundreds of rivers.

She had a smile on her face in all seasons, a sort of eternal spring with permanently lush meadows and plump cattle. Spring, summer, fall, winter, every single day, at all hours, she sang. Like a stream flowing through a desert without losing a drop of water, in fact sounding even crisper, more resonant.

One summer, when everyone was busy with the wheat harvest, they came home to find she'd been so absorbed singing opera in the courtyard that she'd forgotten to make lunch. In a rage, my uncle smashed a dozen plates on the ground. "Now look what you've done," she said, unbothered. "What are the kids going to eat off now?" She sauntered past him, humming, and lit the stove. In between melodies, she called out to him, "So lunch is late today. Is the sky going to fall down?"

Not wanting to delay the harvest, my uncle fumed in the courtyard for a while, then stamped his foot. "Forget it! We'll eat out today!" He led his brood out, promising them a feast. Let's say a bowl of beef and mutton soup each, maybe accompanied by half a steamed bun or flatbread. The prospect of such delectable food made my cousins glad their mother had gotten distracted. Nothing she'd whip up could compare with the spiteful meal their father was offering them. Still holding their scythes and ropes, they followed him. From behind came my aunt-in-law's voice as she ran after them, "Don't forget to bring some back for me! I want mutton soup—"

Then she went back to the village green, smiling and belting out "Who Says Women Don't Know Men" from the Henan opera version of *Hua Mulan*.

When I think back to that time, my aunt-in-law's humming and singing echo in my ears and wind through the village. Just as history is written in annals and achievements are carved on stone tablets, the hardship and bitterness of Eldest Uncle's family were invariably accompanied by those tunes.

Amid this incessant music, their eight children grew up, got married, and established themselves in the world. The needle of time pierced through difficulties, straight through one season after another, all the way into a new century and new era. When we look back now, in our memories we hear a village woman singing in the face of hard times, and we finally understand that it wasn't just her voice she was unleashing, but defiance and strength in the face of life and fate. If not for her steadfast singing and resistance, how could they have survived those harsh winters when all the kids had to squeeze onto the same bed, with only a single blanket over them?

That epoch was over, and a new one had arrived. Visiting Eldest Aunt-in-Law in her newly built house, I asked, "How come you've loved singing all your life?"

"How else would I get through all these days?" She was in her seventies by then. Turning to me and my sisters, she said, "Would you like to hear me sing now?"

We didn't answer, just chuckled. The house was full of life and female laughter. The courtyard, the town, the entire world were submerged in it and rose anew from the waves.

If I had to choose the most heroic, intrepid woman from my entire clan, I think I'd have to vote for Eldest Aunt-in-Law.

Fourth Aunt-in-Law

A lot of the time, when I try to think about the women in my extended family from a woman's point of view, it feels like trying to see the forests or plains from the perspective of a leaf. Trees are just trees, grass is just grass, and nothing about them could change. But when you set aside the rigid gender binary and see them as people who happen to be women, or human beings who have attained womanhood, then they shine and grow resplendent in their full glory. Unfortunately, our clan, our village, and our countryside don't see them like that. That's how my family ended up judging Fourth Aunt-in-Law for being "petty" and "narrow-minded" for "always holding grudges." She was delivered by the matchmaker into the Yan family, so both by random chance and as a matter of destiny she became one of us. Without any effort, Fourth Uncle gained a housekeeper, manager, and accountant. He was attentive to her every instruction, like a leaf moving with the wind and the branch it's attached to. He handed over all his wages to her each month. If she told him to wear blue, he'd never dream of wearing black. And if she decided the gray was better after all, he'd go change—but to him, the gray might as well be the bluest sky. From this perspective, you could say Fourth Aunt-in-Law was the feminist ideal of a village woman. When my uncle retired and they had to decide whether their son or daughter would take over his job in the city, the whole world insisted that it ought to be the son, but Fourth Aunt-in-Law wielded her tongue against the mob and stood up for her daughter—and sure enough, she got dispatched to the city, while the son remained in the village, farming and doing odd jobs. Everyone was confused, but she explained her logic simply: "The boy is strong, so he'll do better at farming and delivering things. How much planting and heavy lifting do you think a girl can manage?"

Fourth Aunt-in-Law might have been illiterate, but she understood all along that "men and women are different types of people." And also that "one is not born but becomes a woman; one is not born but becomes a man." From the point of view of "a person who happens to be female" or "one who has become a woman," she interrogated the universal political ideals of feminism and equality. She was a banner of difference, a mirror to us all, an outlier in our clan. One time, many years ago, my mother stopped speaking to Fourth Aunt-in-Law because of something she'd said. Fourth Aunt-in-Law then ignored my mother too. The sisters-in-law turned a cold shoulder to each other for months on end. Whenever they met, they'd look up at the sky, at the treetops, anywhere but at each other. Then during reform and opening up, most hutong households were either ordered to move to the bustling town center where it would be easier for them to set up a business, or they were deployed to a more remote locale to raise chickens and goats. Our lively hutong was slowly depopulated, leaving no one but a few old folks, including Mother and Fourth Aunt-in-Law.

How could their cold war continue in these circumstances?

But which of them would lower herself to speak first?

I went home that autumn. After giving me a rundown of all the births, illnesses, and deaths in the village, my mother mentioned that the feud with Fourth Aunt-in-Law had deepened. One time, Mother was walking by when Fourth Aunt-in-Law tried to say something, but Mother ignored her. Why? It all started because my mother's son, a famous author, began sending her an allowance. She used the extra cash to plant so many vegetables she had surplus to sell at the market. This humiliated Fourth Aunt-in-Law, and she saw only one way to preserve her dignity: the silent treatment. To my mother, this hurt caused mountains and oceans of resentment. Whenever she walked past Fourth Aunt-in-Law's house, she told me, she always made the first move and never waited for Fourth Aunt-in-Law to start the conversation. Despite Mother's display of humility, Fourth Aunt-in-Law kept finding fault with her, so Mother decided they should stop speaking. "I wasn't about to let her walk all over me, like your fourth uncle does." Fourth Aunt-in-Law's (feminist) temper came from being spoiled by my uncle, she insisted. He'd been useless all his life—why, he had no patriarchal sense at all.

I felt it was my duty to stop the feud. This wasn't just a squabble between two sisters-in-law in their seventies and eighties, but also an archetypal conflict between two "old women" that touched on femininity, women's rights, and human dignity. The next day, while my mother was out, I grabbed the eggs and milk powder someone had given her that she hadn't been able to finish and brought them to Fourth Aunt-in-Law. I found her in her courtyard and handed them over, claiming my mother had sent me and insisted I ask after her. At their age, with so few people left in the hutong, it would be a shame to go on not speaking.

A red glow rose to my aunt's face. Full of excitement and doubt, she glared at me and asked over and over: Did my mother really feel this way? Did she really say all that? Did these things really come from her?

I nodded with as much sincerity as I could muster.

But then my aunt, as either a person who'd become a woman or a woman who'd become a person, asserted her self-respect. She was prepared for this and had thought deeply about her conditions. "If your mother truly wants to mend our relationship, tell her to come for a visit. Let her say a word or two to me first."

"Or *you* could come by and call her sister." I smiled ingratiatingly. "Does it really matter who speaks first?"

Her face hardened. "Of course it matters! Your family is so superior, and you live so much better than us. How could I be the one to speak first?"

I had nothing to say to that.

So we were superior. This superior person stood beneath the autumn sun, at a loss. I thought about how sensitive Fourth Aunt-in-Law must be about her dignity as a woman and a human being, given her life and circumstances, and how important this must be to her. So I agreed that my mother would visit Fourth Aunt-in-Law's home and would speak the first words. After saying goodbye, I stepped out into the deserted street and looked at the sky, at the ground, at the distant hills with their okra plants and the bright sun above. Then I went to the market and bought a crate of absolutely top-notch instant noodles and a carton of Coca-Cola, wandered down another hutong and trampled on fallen leaves that crunched through the silence. Feeling strangely excited, I headed home and found my mother making dumplings for lunch. I placed my purchases in front of her and told her, smugly and triumphantly, that I'd bumped into Fourth Aunt-in-Law outside the hutong, and she'd insisted that I pass my mother these gifts. Also, she'd said the rumors going round the village were absolutely not to be trusted; their neighbors were just trying to drive a wedge between them.

My mother stood in the courtyard, rinsing a bundle of chives, staring at me.

Casually, I nudged the boxes closer to her, opened one of them, and raised a bottle of Coke to my lips.

"I don't believe your fourth aunt-in-law would spend money on me," she said quietly.

"I found it strange too." I examined the bottle. "This tastes like the real thing, like the sort you can buy in Luoyang."

Mother pondered. "Maybe someone gave this to Changke"—Fourth Aunt-in-Law's eldest son—"and she couldn't finish it, so she passed it on to me."

"It's the thought that counts."

My mother was silent for a while. Finally, she muttered to herself that they'd given us a yard, so we had to give them back an inch. Even so, she wanted a goodwill gesture before the thaw, so she tried to dispatch me back to Fourth Aunt-in-Law's place to invite her over for lunch. I pretended to hesitate. She thought we were loaded, I said, and I could hardly go over there empty handed. The noodles and Coke must have cost a hundred yuan, which means I ought to bring a few hundred yuan of stuff. Here was a conundrum. Sometimes the most profound spiritual questions come down to material objects and money, and these practical details take on huge significance. The physical world occupies our spirit, and its chaos fragments and blurs black-and-white questions of gender and dignity. No one understands my mother better than I, and I would bet I understood Fourth Aunt-in-Law best of all too. I'd be so bold as to claim that among the authors working today, you'd be hard-pressed to find one who understands village life and farm folk more thoroughly than I do. Whether as "ones who have become women" or "women who have achieved personhood," my mother and aunt-in-law were as familiar to me as favorite brands and labels are to any shopaholic.

My mother looked as if she were hesitating over whether to buy a familiar local product. I knew she was a great rural mathematician, and after what I'd just said, she'd quickly work out exactly how many cartons of this-or-that a few hundred yuan would buy. Having crunched the numbers, she walked with me in silence to Fourth Aunt-in-Law's home, where she personally invited her sister-in-law to come round for chive and egg dumplings.

After that meal, Mother and Fourth Aunt-in-Law never had another argument. By the time Fourth Aunt-in-Law left this world last March, they'd become so close that they understood, as great intellectuals do, that whether their womanhood or personhood came first, they were human beings first and foremost, and what human beings need above all is understanding and love, not jealousy and separation.

Interlude 7

"Women who are people and people who are women." This feminist idea that speaks of human dignity, freedom, and political ideals is above the pay grade of any male writer. A man discussing feminism is like a burglar taking part in neighborhood watch meetings. In China, though, especially in rural areas, the idea that "women are human beings first and foremost" feels startling and attention-grabbing. In a northern village, especially in more serious settings, calling female people "women" carries a certain vulgar charge. At a solemn official gathering, such as a conversation about promoting someone or giving them a new role, a single high-ranking man only has to say, "Forget it, she's a woman!" for the whole crowd to nod and snort their approval, showing their shared understanding that "a woman is a woman" (and not a person). To this day, it's depressingly common to hear of rural women being subject to domestic violence because they aren't seen as people. Some even regard this as a part of traditional culture, a sad fact of the patriarchy. In the myriad cases of women and girls being kidnapped and sold, despite many attempts by the authorities to stop this practice, we see the victims being valued according to four main criteria: age, health, appearance, and education. In cases of child kidnapping, boys are sold for at least twice as much as girls. In these and many other ways, we see proof that society does not view women as human beings. Even when they are, they're women first and foremost, and only after that can they be people. This confusion allows them to be easily categorized as non-people. As a result, when I see women-run households (like Fourth Aunt-in-Law's), in my own family or elsewhere, I can't help giving them a bit more attention. I want to know whether these women take charge because of male weakness, or simply because they're so strong and capable.

I've never come across a truly equal rural household, nor one where the men are enlightened enough to share power with the women. And I've definitely never encountered a woman who, for explicitly feminist reasons, forces a man to surrender his authority. When I talk about women-run households, I mean it's the women who control the bank accounts, or choose what their home should look like, or decide whether their old folk should be treated with reverence or neglect. It's in these seemingly minor details that we see how the family is run, and hence the position and power of the women within it, which in turn is an indicator of how enlightened and liberated society is in this regard.

To take a wider view, in virtually every household in China, including in the cities, divorced women use various means to wrest power back. In the end, though, the world seems inclined to believe that the patriarchy was bestowed on us by the powers that be. In the small number of households like Fourth Aunt-in-Law's, where the woman holds the reins, it's usually because a "weak" man has ceded power to them. As a result, when a village woman gets married, her mother will secretly tell her not to overly satisfy her husband, not to give his desires too much sway in the marital bed. Leave men wanting more, goes this line of thinking, and they'll do as you say—the only way for a woman to gain stature in the family. This notion that woman must trade their bodily autonomy and sex for power is rooted in the idea that they are non-people. When I look at the situation from this perspective, "sympathetic" as I am toward Fourth Uncle's "plight," I do have to smile approvingly and respectfully at the vague notion that "women are people too" who are "human first, then women," embodied by Fourth Aunt-in-Law in her household and in village society.

I present this praise to Fourth Aunt-in-Law like a bouquet.

She was a practitioner of feminism in a rural Chinese setting, an undefined yet outstanding exemplar. This wasn't just a game to her.

Third Aunt-in-Law

Third Aunt-In-Law was the last "spirit person" in our town, and maybe in a whole swath of the North. Her passing extinguished the final spark of shamanic belief in our village, our town, and maybe even our county. She had a unique mode of being and character, whether as a person or a woman, like an ancient tree on the village green or some mysterious blossom that everyone talked about but few had seen in person.

When your child wouldn't stop sobbing in the night, she'd instruct you to go to a particular tree or telegraph pole at the crossroads in the small hours and put up a yellow charm paper on which you'd written in ink, "By the earth and the sky, make my child no longer cry." If your child had a fever that refused to break no matter what the town doctor did, she'd have you leave the house at midnight with the kid in your arms, heading directly north or west into the freezing wind, right into an icy river (just as in the West, feverish children are treated with ice baths), until a certain hour when you'd come to a building or mountain you couldn't pass, then you should turn around, and your child's fever would dissipate so that the next morning they'd wake up and could be treated with regular medicine.

How could she do this?

Because she was connected to the spirit world!

That wasn't the most astonishing thing about her. What blew me away was something I witnessed many times in my youth, and then again in middle age: her treatment of certain "nervous illnesses." If someone's sickly daughter fell into a melancholic fit, or had some other mental issue, or else if someone in the village had what we called the "sheep horn sickness," that is, epilepsy, if they fell to the ground frothing at the mouth with their teeth chattering, someone would bring them to Third Aunt-in-Law's home, and she'd set three red chopsticks in a white plate so their thick ends touched at the center. Then she'd kneel by the patient, light some incense, and murmur at the chopsticks, "If you're So-and-So, stand up now. If not, keep still"—"So-and-So" being the name of someone in our village who'd recently died, Zhang or Li or Wang or Zhao. The chopsticks wouldn't move at first, but then she'd get to the fourth or fifth name, someone recently deceased or long departed, and the three chopsticks would slowly stir, rising up to stand in the middle of the plate.

The onlookers would gape at this, the heavens would grow still in shock, the mountains fall dumb. And the afflicted person would start mumbling answers to Third Aunt-in-Law's questions. At this point, the patient was no longer themselves but rather the dead person—usually from our village or a nearby one. She'd ask if they didn't have enough warm clothes for the cold weather, of if the grain harvest that year was insufficient, or if their roof was leaking, or if they'd gone to the market only to find they had no money on them. At this point, the deceased person would list in the patient's voice all their needs and problems. Third Aunt-in-Law would reply, "Got it. Off you go, and I'll sort all this out in a day or two."

With that, the red chopsticks would clatter back down onto the plate.

The afflicted person would slowly return to normal and sit up from the ground, look at the crowd and say, "Where am I? I had the strangest dream."

Thus would end another round of "possession." Many such incidents, which Lu Xun called "trickery" or "magic," linger in my memory. The main point is not in the game or trick of possession, but in that Third Aunt-in-Law gave me my earliest, deepest literary inspiration. She taught me that literary lies can become truth if you provide proof. Making the impossible possible requires talent; but the transplanting of possibilities is about literature, not ability. It didn't matter whether these people were actually possessed. The important thing was that Third Aunt-in-Law could make the chopsticks stand upright, providing evidence that allowed spectators to believe this was no game but solid truth.

In the 1990s, I once again witnessed Third Aunt-in-Law raising chopsticks to heal a patient. Sometime this century, I decided that I had to solve the mystery of those chopsticks if I wanted to make a breakthrough in my writing, so one winter day, I visited Third Aunt-in-Law, bearing gifts. I found her on her sickbed by the stove, and our conversation went in circles. "Third Aunt-in-Law," I said, "you have no strength left and you ache all over, and the hospital can't do anything for you, but can't you heal yourself?" "No," she said, "I can't." I asked why not, and she said the heavens wanted to take her away, so what choice did she have? Next,

I asked how she'd made the chopsticks stand upright. She was silent for a while, then she reached out to take my hand and said, "I'm so sorry, Little Ke"—that's what my mother and all my elders called me as a kid. Then, after a pause, she said something astonishing.

"Little Ke," she said. "You're a man. If you were a woman, your third Aunt-in-Law would be happy to tell you how to make chopsticks stand upright on a plate."

"But why?"

"Because men are mortals and women are goddesses," she said, slowly and forcefully. Ever since the heavens and earth were parted, she added, women have been the rulers of this world. It's women who give birth and create this great, populous world. Men are transformed from snake demons, monkey demons, tiger demons, and they've usurped women's celestial positions and earthly thrones, keeping them apart from the divine. Men have strength, wealth, and power, and they were able to subdue the world, setting themselves against and tormenting women. The three-chopstick ritual was the only way women could still connect to the spirit world. As long as anyone was willing to cross the veil, she could make the chopsticks stand. Ordinary people might see nothing but three chopsticks, but she knew they were a bridge to the next world. Whenever she crossed the bridge to speak to the gods, she could help the dead fix any issues with their food or clothing or accommodation. She held my hand through this speech, and now she said again she was sorry, but she truly couldn't tell me the secret. If she told a man, it would block women's last remaining channel to the divine.

Back in the nineties, we burned wood and coal in the winter, but by now most families had electric heaters or used honeycomb charcoal. Yet in Third Aunt-in-Law's tile-roofed house, I heard the crackle of burning wood. As my uncle carefully stoked the fire, she went on speaking vehemently about the mortal and divine worlds. I didn't find any of this ridiculous and didn't feel like laughing once. I listened carefully and decided that when she was done, I would ask her some more probing questions about gods and humans and the universe.

"Are you saying that when the chopsticks stood up, you saw the gods for real?"

She nodded.

"What did you say to them?"

"I complained about men," she said a little hesitantly, eyeing my uncle and letting go of my hand. She looked up at the ceiling and the lights, then went on blandly, "You men have wrecked the world. Government officials bully common people, and those officials are all men. The people selling counterfeits in the street are greedy men. And yes, plenty of women are involved in kidnapping and trafficking women and children, but their bosses are all men. Men send women to do their dirty work. Every evil thing in the world is done by men. Women only get involved if men make them do it."

She was in such despair she couldn't go on. All this thinking seemed to have worn her out. I wanted to ask more about men being the source of all evil, a point of view you hardly ever heard among regular folk, but she had fallen asleep. Thus ended a distinctive, profound conversation about gender. Sleep closed the door on gods, humans, the universe, and the unknown. Regretfully, I left. Third Uncle walked me out. At the doorway, I asked about what Third Aunt-in-Law just said, and he pointed out something else: "Did you notice the dead souls she raised with her chopsticks were always men, never women?" His explanation was Third Aunt-in-Law believed men were much worse than women, greedy for food and sex and money and nicer housing, and when they faced the slightest discomfort in the nether world, they immediately turned to possession to fix it. And it was often young women's bodies they sought to inhabit, like the lechers they were. As my uncle finished telling me how men were the root of all bad things, his kid called him to come inside, so I said goodbye.

The future lies ahead of us, but the gods and the universe are somewhere else. We live on this tiny ball of dirt, lonely and bleak. Will it be the gods or the universe that controls our future? Who should I plumb the mysteries of the unknown universe with? Are literature and art made by human beings or by the divine? All these doors have quietly closed in my face. Third Aunt-in-Law telling me that men are the source of all evil in the world made me reevaluate my perspective and value system as a male author. In order to keep sorting through my thoughts and feelings, I thought, the next time I visited Third Aunt-in-Law, I would bring one of my sisters or my sister-in-law. As women and victims of the patriarchy, they may be able to get Third Aunt-in-Law to reveal the secret of the chopsticks to them, then they too would have a feminine connection to the divine. As well as complaining about men to the gods, they could also help me ask about the future, the unknown, the arts, and our place in the universe.

I'd also love to know exactly what gripes Third Aunt-in-Law shared about men while she was there.

Unfortunately, I never got round to asking my female relatives to quiz Third Aunt-in-Law. A few years ago, as spring was turning into summer, Third Aunt-in-Law went over to the side of the gods, taking her secrets with her. All she left was her harsh, insistent declaration that men are the source of all evil, looming like a mountain ridge in front of me, crushing the pen in my hand like a book that's been dropped into a shredder.

5
Mother

Language and Thought

My mother gets a whole chapter to herself because she's my mother.

As a child, I thought my mother was a woman of few words, but everything she said was true. In middle age, I found her quiet, even inarticulate. These days, I think she's a very good speaker with her own brand of logic, and whatever subject she chooses, she brings her own style and thought process to it.

Turns out this so-called life arises out of language. When my mother wants to say something is large, she calls it "as big as the world." If it's small, she says, "The size of a person's heart." When someone's tall, "his hair is brushing the sky." And for a bad-tempered person, "Pigs and dogs don't go boo when they see him."

Fifteen years ago, the doctors found shadows on my mother's lungs. My wife and sister-in-law took her to three different hospitals in Beijing. The latter two said the shadows might not be tumors but rather scar tissue from an earlier bout of tuberculosis. We rushed to my mother's ward with the news that the first doctor had been wrong, and everything was okay now. As we rejoiced, my mother took the diagnosis, which she couldn't read, and stared at it for a long time before carefully asking, "Was the first one definitely wrong?"

"Yes, definitely."

"Then the hospital should give us our money back. They were the ones who made a mistake. They made us live in fear for a whole month. In fact, they ought to pay us damages."

This was unassailable logic, tight as the bond between sky and land. Still, to celebrate my mother being cancer-free, we decided not to demand a refund or compensation from the first hospital. We sorted out the paperwork to get my mother discharged, and at 1 p.m. the next day, we got a flight to Sanya for a vacation. This was my mother's first time on a plane, so we gave her the window seat. She glanced out and said, "One year, the cotton harvest was whiter than these clouds." When a bout of turbulence shook the plane, I grabbed her arm, but she calmly said, "It's fine, cars hit bad patches of road too." By the time we were done talking about clouds, cotton, and roads, it was time for lunch. I told my mother, "This meal is free. The airline is giving it to us." My mother stared at the box of food and thought about it. "How could there be such a thing as a free lunch? I bet they made the tickets more expensive to cover the cost, and now they're claiming there's no charge. At the end of the day, you're spending money and they're earning it." She scanned my face for confirmation. I gave it some thought and solemnly nodded. "That's possible," I said. "It really is possible."

We kept chatting, while also pondering the various traps and survival mechanisms in our lives and the world. Then we began our descent into Sanya.

We were staying at a military hotel on the coast. After checking in, we hurried to see the ocean before it got dark. This was Mother's first sight of the sea, though she told us that she was just a few years old when she heard that this world contained a thing known as the ocean. She knew it took up more space than the land—she'd learned that the earth's proportions were "three parts mountain, six parts water, one part flatland." The sun was setting, sending its last rays over the sandy beach. As my comrades and I led Mother through the hotel doors, she stopped in shock, her face full of surprise and excitement. As she gaped at the ocean, she said something only someone of her abilities could have come up with: "Oh my God. That's far too much water!"

We helped her through a flower garden down to the beach. She let some sand run through her fingers and looked down the long coastline. "If this sand were grain, no one would ever go hungry again." Gazing at the seagulls flapping tirelessly between sea and sky, she said, "Silly things. If there's nothing to do, you should rest. What are they flying around for?" My comrades had booked us a private room at a restaurant for a welcome dinner. Staring at the table laden with all kinds of seafood and other dishes, my mother pulled me aside and whispered, "Are you sure we won't need to pay for this?" I told her, "My army buddy is a regiment leader. That's like being a county chief or the director-general of a bureau. He can sign for our room and board, and it'll all be comped."

Mother stood in a corner of that private room and said a simple sentence that I've spent half my life thinking about: "Being a government official—now, there's a good thing."

Dusk faded away and night arrived.

Nighttime in Sanya felt completely different than on the plains back up north. In our village, darkness arrived in clumps, and the moon hung serenely in the sky. Once a month, it would be as round as a painting from the divine, blurred and speckled from the careless swipe of a god's brush. On that southern autumn night in Sanya, just 3,000 kilometers from the equator, the moonlight had the golden sheen of the summer sun, looming over us like a fire that gave off cold air. From the hotel balcony, the sky was the color of white satin fresh off the loom. Finding the merest defect amid this paleness felt like an enormous discovery. And yet, how bland this sky seemed, without a single speck of any other color. Such a vast ocean. Its roaring in the night made up for the monotonous sky. By the chilly, golden glow of the moon, the sea roiled from the horizon to the shore, and the rush of its waves battered the windows, as if someone were banging on the glass calling you, keeping their voice down so as not to wake anyone else, just hoarse cries and muffled thuds.

The moonlight and the waves woke me up.

I turned to check on my mother. By the moonlight, I saw that not only was her bed empty, but her blanket was neatly folded as it had been at the start of the night. I glanced toward the bathroom, but it was inky dark, a black wall. Where was Mother? As I formulated the question, an image filled my mind: a tsunami rushing onto the shore, sweeping away the people and buildings in its path, heading straight for me. With a shock I jumped out of bed and sprinted from the room without getting dressed. Down the stairs, through the lobby, out the door, toward the sea. I ran through the garden, all the way to the beach, and there was Mother on the shore, staring at the expanse of water, her back to the land, unmoving and mesmerized by the glimmers of gold on the ever-shifting surface. She looked like she had been sculpted from sand, like she was melting into the moonlight.

I slowed down. When I reached Mother, I sat next to her.

"Aren't you afraid the waves will carry you away?" I said quietly.

She turned and stared at me for a moment, before saying in a tone of wonder, "How is there so much water?" She looked at the sea, then at the sky and reddish moon in that infinite expanse, then back to the hazy blue ocean and its silver-white ripples, weighing her words. "Lianke, do you think there really is a god in this world? If not, how could there be day and night, sun and moon, seas and mountains? But if God is real, how could God be so unfair? There's more water here than anyone could need, while our village is short of water to drink or water our crops. The trees here have such fat leaves and flowers so big they look fake. But in the North, I've been to Xi'an and Lintong in Shaanxi, where the farmers don't even have houses, they live in caves. Their crops long for rain like a child waits for his mother to come home. If God is so good, he could have sent more water to places that need it and put more roads through the mountains in the first place. And he could send fewer floods and hurricanes to people who live near the water.

Why does it have to be this way? Some places have a lot of this and not enough of that, and elsewhere it's the other way round."

With that, she returned to her observation of the gleaming sea, the desolate earth, and the cavernous sky, waiting for my reply as if she were waiting for the ocean to run dry. But how could I answer this question about the origin of humanity and injustices of the world? My mother is not just a linguistics expert, she's also a philosopher and thinker as unafraid to face reality as Socrates himself. As for me, I'm just her foolish, cowardly, and ignorant pupil and child.

Literacy and Travel

If anyone says my mother is illiterate, *they're* the illiterate one.

My mother is educated. Fairly well educated. Even if we take the narrow definition of "educated" to mean how many words she knows and how many books she's read, I think her ability to recognize words is still astounding.

How many words does she know?

Statistics are inherently silly, even though some people believe science and accuracy are built on a foundation of statistics, just as in Greek mythology the wind god Aeolus blew a gust and timed its return so he could gauge how far he would have to walk as a mortal. Here's what I will say about my mother: However many words her life has required her to learn, that's how many words she knows. That's my second sister's evaluation of my mother, and it's as accurate as detecting when rain is on the way.

Back when she had to add up work points for the production brigade, my mother taught herself the Arabic numerals 1 to 10. There was always a piece of chalk on the stone column by our front door, where she kept her records: tabulating our family's work points and grain allocation every season, a three-pointed or five-pointed star to mark when the summer or autumn harvest was abundant.

A square meant a perfectly regular year, ordinary as trees sprouting to life in spring, regardless of how the harvest had been.

I joined the army at the end of 1978, and in early 1979 my mother learned to write her name, Zhou Lingxian, comprising three ancient characters imbued with the hopes of the people. When I asked why she learned, she said when I started sending money home in January, she went to the post office to make a withdrawal and had to sign for it. The clerk wrote my mother's name on a sheet of paper so she could copy the words onto the slip. After a couple of times, she could do it without copying. Not only that, she could recognize (but perhaps not write) the characters for Song County, Tianhu, Yan Lianke, Yan Fa'ke (my brother), Yan Sujing (Big Sis) and Yan Sufen (Second Sis). Whenever she went to Luoyang and had to get back to Tianhu, she used to ask people which bus to take. One time, she asked a middle-aged bespectacled man who didn't answer her, just glared at her and glanced up before walking off. Then she realized she was standing right next to her bus, and the words "Song County" were in bright red directly overhead. She no longer blamed the passerby for ignoring her and decided she would make it her business to learn the words for "Song County" and "Tianhu," as well as the names of her children and their children. My niece, who lived with her, taught her a new character every day, and soon she knew them all.

She's also learned a few other characters. In order to know which toilet to use, she's had to learn the words for "Male" (男—"he has a bent leg") and "Female" (女—"two crossed legs"). She also learned "Luoyang," "Henan," and "China," which felt to me as aspirational as Yue Fei's mother carving "Serve Your Country with Utmost Loyalty" into her son's skin. When I asked her why she needed to know these words, she chuckled and said "Song County" and "Tianhu" were enough to bring her home from Luoyang, but what if the day came when I took her to Beijing, Guangzhou, or Shenzhen? Or Hong Kong, Taiwan, Japan, or elsewhere? Best to learn "Henan" and "China" well in advance of that.

Turns out my mother was waiting for me to take her farther afield. To Japan, South Korea, Singapore, and maybe even to the US, England, or France. Unfortunately, I wasn't filial enough. Two years ago, I took her and my sisters to Hong Kong, and we spent a week pushing her around in a wheelchair, but we haven't been anywhere beyond that. Whenever I leave the country, no matter where to, I always take plenty of pictures and bring them back to the village called Tianhu, where I carry my stool out to the courtyard and sit next to her, and together we look at photos of Tokyo Tower, the Mongolian steppe, Versailles, the British Museum, the Statue of Liberty, and the fifteen-story-high statue of Christ the Redeemer on Mount Corcovado in Rio de Janeiro's Tijuca National Park. One time, maybe in the spring or summer, there were patches of cloud overhead and silence all around us. I heard a bird chirp in our poplar tree, warm and earthy. My mother said to me, "The world is so large, and I've been to Hong Kong, so my life has been worthwhile."

My sisters and brother arrived then, and so did some neighbors. They always wanted me to bring back autographed books from overseas, to read and because they made better gifts for their coworkers and bosses than cigarettes or liquor. As I distributed the books, my mother took the thickest one from my hands and weighed it up. "I'm old and I can't read. You've written so many books, and I can't make out a single line in any of them. If I'd known what you were going to do for a living, I'd have learned more words while I was still young, just so I could know what you're writing about."

There were tears in her eyes. My siblings smiled and said nothing. My neighbors and cousins loudly mocked her, "You can't read and you've managed to visit so many places. Imagine if you *could* read, you'd have gone clear across the whole universe by now."

Interlude 8

After Zhao Shuli's short story "The Marriage of Young Blacky" became a classic of Chinese political art, what became known as "yokel literature" slapped on some greasepaint and took to the stage across the land, in villages and city streets everywhere, with Third Fairy becoming the ultimate villainess, the thorn of syphilis in China's wedding culture. But to look at this impartially, if marriage is an essential part of human life—for reproduction, survival, sex, and love—then how could we continue to exist without matchmakers?

You could say that matchmakers are the greatest supporters and motivators of Chinese marriage culture. But our language, art, and drama have successfully popularized the term "matchmaking granny," which shears away the matchmaker's qualities of bringing together and bonding and instead highlights negative stereotypes such as glibness, hypocrisy, and selfishness. The dissemination of this term was a profound, carefully designed act of propaganda. Through print, stage, and other media, it has been implanting this idea in our mind since ancient times. The predecessors of today's matchmakers were known as "red women"; in verse and on stage, they would typically receive veneration and gratitude from young couples they'd saved from despair. For instance, the Tang poet Wang Huan's *Twelve Melancholic Poems* includes the lines "Silk sheets wrap the lovers, at midnight they share a pillow. The clock chimes and the red woman urges her to leave. She sheds tears on her gold hairpin." The Song dynasty poet Liu Kezhuang's "River of Crimson" asks, "And who is able to wait in the moonlight for the red woman bearing a message?" And in the anonymous "Huanxi Sands," we have: "Red women dance in tattered dresses. Rouge like a palace, dew on branches."[1] All examples of sorrowful, respectful farewells to red women. In *Romance of the Western Chamber*, Cui Yingying's maid is named "Hongniang," which means "red woman"—she's the origin of the term, as she not only plays the most important role in bringing the young couple together, one could argue she's also the hero in this tale of star-crossed love. The same goes for Yue Fei and Xin Qiji, writing as the empire fell apart around them.

When *Romance of the Western Chamber* was adapted for the stage, it was simply and resonantly titled *Hongniang*, further establishing the archetype of the female matchmaker. By the time of Yan'an literature and "The Marriage of Young Blacky," though, a further evolution had taken place: The matchmaker was now an older lady. The red women were erased, along with the respect they inspired, leaving only the matchmaking granny to be ridiculed and belittled. To see how this villainous figure continued proliferating, you could look at *The Water Margin*, particularly Yan Poxi in Chapter 20, "The Brothel-Keeper While Drunk Strikes Tang Niu-er; Song Jiang While Angry Kills the Girl Yan Poxi," and Chapters 23, "Grandma Wang Being Covetous Spoke Seductively; Yun Ge Makes a Row in a Tea Shop," through to Chapter 26, "The Night Witch Sells a Man's Flesh at Mengzhou; Wu Song Meets Zhang Qing at the Crossroads."[2] And today, now that *The Golden Lotus* has been admitted by many scholars into the canon, its exquisite depiction of Grandma Wang can be said to be the clearest and most successful illustration of the move from "matchmaker" to "matchmaking granny." The appearance of this figure in "Young Blacky" isn't just a callback to Grandma Wang. The figure of Third Fairy was imbued with the overwhelming forces of revolution and politics and hence took root in society and in our hearts far more effectively than Grandma Wang or Yan Poxi in *The Golden Lotus* or *The Water Margin*. If anyone were to go through *Romance of the Western Chamber*, *The Water Margin*, *The Golden Lotus* all the way to "Young Blacky," and chart the evolution of the "red woman," "matchmaker," and "matchmaking granny," while also investigating the resonances and overlaps of these terms with literature, the arts, history, and politics, they'd surely find that this wasn't just a question of a shifting archetype but rather that these changes were in concert with or caused by historical and political developments. Going back to the Yuan dynasty, we see that Wang Shifu had the utmost respect and praise for women, while bringing a deep historical perspective to his critique on the stifling of love. By the time of *The Water Margin*, however, this understanding and tolerance has been shattered by the unyielding patriarchal mindset. There is a lot of enthusiasm for research into *The Golden Lotus* today, because academics are interested in the individual pursuit—especially by women—of liberation and bodily autonomy. Then we come to "Young Blacky," where revolution has replaced the liberatory impulse, abandoning the delicate and respectful portrayal of women in *Western Chamber* in favor of a class-based binary in which people are either good or bad, particularly in the case of Third Fairy, the matchmaking granny of Little Qin.

The perspective most easily spread and accepted is this binary, black-and-white one, rather than a more nuanced, three-dimensional view of our place in the world. We see this most starkly in China, with notions such as "anything that isn't revolutionary is antirevolutionary." Thus when "Young Blacky" makes use of revolutionary fervor to push past the literary realm into the arena of class and revolution, the effect is not only to shift the archetype from "matchmaker" to "matchmaking granny," but also to bury the tradition of benevolent love and respect for women that came with the "red woman." Even today, although matchmakers (mostly women) still exist in the real world, the mocking of this stereotype has not diminished.

That said, we now have new terms such as "marriage broker," which shows a continued understanding and respect for marriage, an institution and social order human beings can't seem to get away from. There are also three further layers of significance. Firstly, while red women, matchmakers, and matchmaking grannies all tended to be female, "broker" is a gender-neutral term. Secondly, brokers are not seen as figures to be either lauded or criticized but more accurately as agents who are simply responsible for introducing two people to each other. Finally, there's an openness to this term that is in keeping with evolving norms. This social role has been known by different words, each replacing the one before it, in tandem with the way women in China have been treated and viewed across thousands of years. By studying this shifting vocabulary, we can easily see the shifts in the positioning of women in literature, art, and history.

Matchmaker

Among the many roles my mother has played in her life, one is often forgotten: matchmaker.

Where we're from in the Central Plains, matchmakers are envied and looked up to. They're always respectably dressed and well-spoken, and they act decisively. Village matchmaker is not a profession but a crucial moral function in society. No matchmaker doing it for the money could sustain that for long. Their objective is to forge connections between two households, and to be responsible to them for the rest of their lives. Any matchmaker worth their salt would be familiar with both parties' social standing, family members, household income, personality traits, neighborly relationships, and so on, to judge the likelihood that a pair of strangers might come to know each other, get married, have kids, and grow old together. I don't know who the first couple were that my mother brought together, but I remember that whenever a local got hitched with much bustle and commotion, my mother would often be celebrating too. She'd stand out from the gaudily dressed crowd because, over the freshly laundered outfit she wore to fetch the bride, she'd have a red satin sash around her waist, which marked her as the person who'd introduced this husband and wife: their matchmaker.

The births, illnesses, deaths, weddings, and widowings of our neighbors in and around our villages and among our neighbors are the most important beginnings and endings in rural life, part of the cycle of seasons and renewals in the lives of villages and individuals. When someone died, my mother would sew an outfit for them to be buried in. When they got married, she would be asked to receive the bride. And if she happened to be their matchmaker too, then at some point after the wedding, the young couple, flushed bright red and smiling shyly, would show up at our house with a little something. Not money. Maybe apples, walnuts, peanuts, or whatever was ripe that season, persimmons or grapes. My mother would accept what they brought, but she'd be obliged to send them away with something too, invariably also peanuts, dried persimmons, walnuts, or seasonal fruit.

The spoils of these ritualized visits were the only "income" of a matchmaker. When she saw the Henan opera of "The Marriage of Young Blacky," its action transplanted to Henan, my mother's response was, "Writers come up with such nonsense!" But "Young Blacky" describes events prior to 1949, while my mother's matchmaking experience is all from after this date.

Times have changed.

I don't know when my mother began matchmaking, nor do I know precisely when she stopped. Many of the people in our village, especially our friends, relatives, and immediate neighbors, still talk about "Second Aunt-in-Law" (my mother) facilitating their marriages. Almost all my cousins met their mates through her. Afterward, they'd come by to visit from time to time, in a spirit of gratitude when things were going well, and to complain about their partners when they weren't. In the latter case, when faced with a sobbing man or woman, my mother would respond, "How could they do that!" Then she'd abandon her dinner and drag the visitor back to their spouse.

Her face would be etched with anger and worry when she set off, and perfectly serene when she returned.

"What happened?" my father would say.

"We talked it through. They agreed to get on with each other."

From which I'd understand that yet another household's loose screws had been tightened by my mother. These days, we look at the divorce rates of city people as an indicator of civilization—it's almost as if we believe more divorces means a more enlightened society. In rural villages, though, divorce continues to be seen as a terrible thing. As a result, I can't tell whether my mother should be called conservative or progressive in her views on marriage. Still, she has contributed to the stability and preservation of village life. If anyone had the interest and resources to put together a museum of rural marriage in China, the section devoted to our village should reserve a place for my mother. You couldn't separate her from the unions of all eight of Eldest Uncle's children, six boys and two girls. At various points she has been the red woman or the matchmaker, as well as occasionally playing the villainess Third Fairy.

Eldest Aunt-in-Law was always singing, singing, singing. She'd brought her children into this world and made sure they could speak and walk, therefore her duty was done, and my uncle was then in charge of making sure they got married and established their careers. One day, my uncle burst into our home and told my parents his sons were grown, and he had to build them houses so they could get married. He could handle the construction, but the task of finding them wives fell squarely on my mother's shoulders.

A year later, my uncle had built three tile-roofed houses. This was the early 1970s, and it felt as if he'd coaxed brightly colored flowers from the barren soil. Alas, these were flowers with withered, malnourished stems and roots. The jade-green tiles were neatly laid and beautiful to look at, and anyone who passed by would stop in their tracks and crane their necks to gawp. The large interiors, however, had hardly any furniture, not even a stool, apart from the obligatory Chairman Mao portrait on the wall. One lunchtime, I saw Uncle come by with his rice bowl. In the lush courtyard of early summer, I overheard his conversation with my parents, which has lingered in my mind to this day.

"The houses are built," he said to my mother. "Now you're in charge of finding wives for them."

My mother nodded solemnly and promised she would take care of her nephews' marriages and lives. Then they ate their lunch and said many more things. After Uncle left, my mother said to my father, "There's nothing at all inside those houses."

"You'll think of something."

"Like what?"

"When a woman comes for a visit, borrow some furniture and stick it in there."

My mother glared at him. "So you want to cheat some poor girl?"

He got serious too. "These are our nephews you're talking about."

The idea of doing this for "our nephews" made Mother abandon her principles, and so she allowed herself to slip from "matchmaker" to "matchmaking granny." She didn't say another word that afternoon. The next day, she set off to make the rounds of nearby villages. Same on the third day. By the fourth or fifth day, she was back to announce that she'd found a young woman named Lian from Xiejiagou village, who'd agreed to meet Uncle's eldest son, and she'd be coming for a visit to Uncle's house the next day. That earth-shattering day quickly came. The day before had ended like all the previous ones, and this day arrived the same as always. Who knew if the sun was the same, or if the new day had brought a different orb? The village was clearly the same village, yet I stubbornly believed it had been renewed. The slanting rays of sun contained both lingering warmth and a hint of chill. People poured into the village from outside, and the courtyards filled with the barley-like aroma of ripe corn, these fragrances mingling to produce something crisp and sweet, as if syrupy saccharin were permeating the air.

The sun rose.

We swung into action.

My mother was the conductor of this wedding scam. She planned and directed the whole thing. At the time, every villager knew *The Art of War* inside out: "Know yourself and know your enemy, and you can fight a hundred battles without defeat." Mother sent Second Sister to Eldest Uncle's house to help Eldest Aunt-in-Law and our cousins with the scrubbing and cleaning. The women and mops and water and rags soon removed every speck of dust. Even the soil outside was gleaming. Tables, chairs, and benches were moved from our home to theirs. Those three tile-roofed houses now had all the furniture they ought to. Wherever a chair should be, there it was, its back painted red. Borrowed pitchers and tea trays were laid out on long tables like display items. Someone's shiny washbasin and rack had made the journey to hang from a corner of the main room. There was a curtain across the doorway to the inner rooms. The old blanket had been replaced by new bedding. The dusty Chairman Mao portrait was now a magnificent poster of five glorious leaders: Marx, Engels, Lenin, Stalin, and Mao.

The world had been transformed.

My cousin, awaiting his would-be bride, was a new person too. He stood in the courtyard in a brand-new uniform, smiling uneasily. His outfit was borrowed, yet it fit perfectly, as if it had been tailored for him.

Everyone on their street was in a frenzy of expectation, and like in a play, the setting and light shifted as time marched on. Past eleven o'clock, with lunchtime approaching, my cousin's almost-fiancée appeared on the road west of the village. With my mother leading the way, half the village saw the young woman's capable, brisk figure coming into view. Someone called out, "She's here! She's here!" and ran out into the street for a better look. "It's the bride!"

Unexpectedly, my future cousin-in-law stood her ground and bellowed, "What the hell do you think you're staring at?"

We froze, all but deafened by her shouting. She was a spicy one. We took a step back as my mother beamed and led her down the road to my uncle's home.

My mother, in her role as matchmaking granny, helped to deceive this woman. The newly built tile-roofed house was fully furnished, spick-and-span, and had the full set of leaders—benevolent, noble Marx, Engels, Lenin, Stalin, and Mao—to welcome and wish her well. All of that, added to my cousin's clean-cut good looks, set this misbegotten marriage chugging down its tracks. I have no idea what the couple talked about when they were left alone, but the woman agreed to marry my cousin. Not only that, when my mother and aunt started discussing garments and bride-gifts, she stunned them all by saying the clothes and presents weren't important. Her family was building a new house so her elder brother could find a wife, and they hadn't found enough artisans or laborers to work on the faraway site.

When the time came, she hoped the Yan family could lend a hand.

With that, the curtain fell on a matchmaking session stuffed with drama and falsehoods.

My uncle's first and third sons happened to be top-notch bricklayers. A few days after the engagement, the family set off in full force to help the woman's clan build their house. After that was done and her brother had tied the knot, she joined our family as Cousin Lian.

Their wedding took place the spring after their engagement. The next day, they came by to see my parents. Unexpectedly, my mother chose this moment to drop her matchmaking granny persona, transforming in the blink of an eye into a red woman. Eagerly, she took hold of Cousin Lian's hand and said, "You're married now. Such a lovely couple. Now the rice is cooked and cannot be uncooked, I have something to tell you." She then revealed that my uncle wasn't as wealthy as she'd made out, and all the furniture that first day had been borrowed. She hoped Cousin Lian would forgive her, she said.

Even more dramatically, after my mother had finished her self-criticism, Cousin Lian didn't show the least sign of anger or upset. Instead, she burst out laughing and said, "Well, obviously. As soon as I stepped in the door, I knew the furniture was someone else's. What kind of family could be rich enough to own all that stuff? And if they were, why on earth would they want *me* for a bride?" Her smile vanished and she gave my mother an odd look. "Second Aunt-in-Law, the first time you came to our house, a lot of our stuff was borrowed from the neighbors. Did you really not notice?"

Then she started chuckling again. "Looks like we're a good match! Furniture, décor, clothes—all borrowed. Same with you, right?"

So the matchmaking granny and matchmaker's roles mingled, like the changing times mixing a basin of water and a bucket of milk together. At certain moments, cheating and lying can create a sort of fairy tale, and may even be a virtue, just as many catastrophes throughout history have produced heroes.

My Mother and Her Uncle and Father

It would be wrong of me to present my mother solely as a high-minded, forthright, and sanguine figure. She's not just my mother, but other people's too. Along with her virtues, I have to mention that she's unsophisticated, shortsighted, and overly fond of complaining. The characters Lu Xun never tired of criticizing, such as Auntie Xianglin, Mother Hua, or "the people asleep in the iron house," have quite a bit in common with my mother.

When she was seventeen, my mother married from Yaodian village, a few kilometers away, to our home. Her mother died when she was not yet one year old. Her father then remarried and started a new family, so she was forced to live with her feeble-minded uncle. She was just a few years old when she started cooking and cleaning for him. Her uncle wasn't able to do anything except farming and eating. Even cooking a pot of rice was an enormous challenge for him. From the age of two or three, he and my mother became "a family."

Then when she was sixteen, he got in the way of an elm tree someone was cutting down, leaving her with nothing but some bloodstained ground and silence. And so fate left her with no choice but to get married at the age of seventeen. She accepted her destiny, which has led me to believe that you could work hard all your life and still not escape whatever arrangements and decisions fate has made for you. If not for that falling elm tree, how long would her uncle had lived? If he'd made it to sixty or seventy, who would my mother have married instead, and would she have ended up any happier? If she'd married into a different village, a different family, or a different fate, where would my siblings and I be?

A single elm tree being cut down decided the course of my mother's life, and therefore also the births and fates of me, my brother, and my sisters. Pursuing this line of thought, you'd conclude that the entire world is run by pure chance. Inevitability is just one small screw in the great machine of fate. As far back as I can remember, since I was maybe four or five or six or seven, my mother would say pretty much every day, "If only my silly uncle were alive today!" Like Auntie Xianglin, she was always asking people, "Do you think when someone dies, they have a soul that lives on?" Or "I was so foolish. I knew that when it snows, wild animals in the hills have nothing to eat and come into the village—but I didn't know that could happen in the springtime too." I grew up amid my mother's Auntie Xianglin–esque mutterings and complaints. The difference was, Auntie Xianglin's words fell on stony ground, as if it wasn't just Lu Xun but also everyone around her who found her tiresome. (I suspect Lu Xun himself would have been quite annoying in real life too.) Whereas my mother's nagging and grumbling left my father, my siblings, and me with tears in our eyes.

It was her family's tears that kept my mother warm.

I don't know what my father was thinking, but at one point he decided to bring this grandfather we'd never met to come live with us. My mother's feeble-minded uncle might no longer be around, but he wanted my mother to know her father was still in this world, so she could feel more like other married women—that she'd sprung from a family. I was eight or nine when I came home from school one day in early spring to find a scrawny, white-haired man with a white beard sitting in our courtyard, dressed in a black tunic, black winter trousers, and black cloth shoes, eating a pocket egg my mother had made him, snow white and golden. My parents stood before him, and the tears in their eyes didn't hide their excitement and joy. The black-clad man's skeletal face likewise shone with tears and glowed with exhilaration.

I froze in the gateway. My parents told me to come over and say hello to "Grandpa." That's when I learned I had an actual grandpa, not just a feeble-minded guy who was no longer around. I timidly walked up to the man and said, "Grandpa." He pulled me to his chest, and his tears plopped into the bowl with the egg in it.

After a gap of over twenty years, my mother began seeing her father regularly.

Now she had a family of her own.

Me and my siblings had acquired a new grandpa, grandma, and uncles.

After this, Mother stopped her Auntie Xianglin questions about souls and comments about wild animals in the spring.

And on the fifth and tenth of every month, on market day, she'd go out at a particular time when the sun was high overhead, find her father in the crowd, and bring him home for a few eggs before sending him out to browse the stalls. Then at noon, he'd come by again and she'd make him a bowl of fine wheat noodles.

For almost a decade, twice a month, my grandpa would drop by his daughter's home while claiming he was just in town for the market. And my mother would also say she was out for market day, but she'd stand by the village green waiting for her father to show up, and her smile when she caught sight of him was one of pure happiness. Her joy at having a father filled the pit of loneliness in her life.

My Mother and My Niece

Both my sisters were married, my brother had a job in the city, and I was in my barracks in Shangqiu, East Henan. As the saying goes, birds fly when they are fledged, sons leave when they are grown. During those long years as empty nesters, my mother and my sickly father lived alone in our tile-roofed house with the courtyard that was invariably breezy in summer and warm in winter. Then in 1984, a year of not much historical significance, my father departed from this world.

That was a difficult year for my family, and yet another disastrous turning point in my mother's fate. It appeared that as a woman, my mother had been born to suffer isolation, and loneliness would cling to her all her life. With my father's passing, the powers that be removed every scrap of air and every bit of movement from all the rooms in our home. We felt the change whenever we stepped into the courtyard or house—it was hard to breathe, as if the world had become an arid vacuum, with shackles and suffocation everywhere. Only the natural order of family feeling and companionship could allow human life to continue contentedly. Without this warmth, we might as well be living without air or water. Particularly in China, where the family unit is often our only source of love and the desire to go on living. Now my father was gone, my mother's sole support had crumbled away.

We buried my father. Afterward, my sisters had to return to their families, and my brother and sister-in-law had to go back to their city jobs. One winter evening, as silence rushed into the courtyard and descended like an enormous, airtight shroud, draping over our home, I watched my mother alone in the kitchen making dinner and keenly sensed the bitterness of the instant my father stopped breathing and she flung herself over him, sobbing, "It's over! The sky is falling!" I understood why my sisters and sister-in-law decided that my elder sister's three-year-old daughter, Yuanyuan, ought to come live with my mother for a while.

Loneliness had been my mother's companion longer than anyone else. When her uncle was at work in the fields, she would make his lunch and wait at the village entrance for him to return, but the way his mind worked, so long as he hadn't finished hoeing a field, he would keep going while the sun passed the meridian, toiling till way past lunchtime, until my mother, tired of sitting on a rock and gazing at the distant, unknowing fields, came looking for him. Then for over a decade after she was married, virtually no one from her birth family came to see her until that day when her father showed up and they embraced in tears, and after that she could watch for him in the crowd every market day.

Now my father had gone ahead of her, and the only person keeping her company was a little ignorant girl who did nothing all day but gnaw at her fingernails, just like my mother at the age when she started living with her uncle. That night was unusually cold, and as the north wind rose, you could hear it ripping scrub from the ground and hurling it against buildings and trees as it howled. In the main room, my father's picture stood alongside his mother's picture on the long table. My mother and my three-year-old niece huddled around the firepit in the inner room, where we spent most of our time because the other rooms were so cold. It felt transgressive abandoning my father to the outer cold, so we arranged his and my grandmother's pictures on a chair nearby. It felt as if he were warming himself by the fire with us, just like the old days.

The room was quiet except for the satiny whooshing sound of rising flames.

The air seemed to be having a conversation with my father.

My niece sat on my lap and my mother across from us. I recalled New Year's Eve a couple of years ago, when my father had his left arm around another granddaughter, Fangfang, while Yuanyuan, just a few months old then, was nestled in his right. Out of nowhere he said, without quite seeming to mean it, "What a good life. I don't know how much longer I'll be able to keep holding these two kids." And now he couldn't hug his granddaughters any longer. I was in his place by the fireside, holding my niece as if she were a magnificent gift that God had bestowed on our household, in warmth and silence, yet there was also desolation and emptiness here. My niece abruptly grabbed her grandfather's picture, held it to her chest, and said something only she could have come up with, "I want Granddad to come to bed with me."

Mother and I both turned to look at her. Mother said the cruelest possible thing: "Your granddad isn't here. He's decided that he isn't going to talk to us or sit with us any longer."

My niece stared at her in shock. I wasn't sure if she'd understood. "That's okay," she said. "If he's not here, I'll hold his photo until he comes back."

That night, the outer room was so cold, my mother invited my father's portrait into the inner room, to her bedside, where it spent the night wrapped in a pillowcase. The next morning, when the sun's familiar warmth seeped into the house, she placed the picture back on the long table to bask in its rays.

After that, whenever Mother felt lonely, she'd try to fill the void with Father's picture. After some time, when my niece noticed her grandmother staring besottedly at her grandfather's face, she'd take her by the hand and lead her gently away, chattering about this or that to distract her.

My niece grew up alongside her grandmother and understood what it meant to depend on another person. Anyone who hasn't had these experiences or emotions will reach maturity like my mother's feeble-minded uncle, refusing to come home for lunch because of an unhoed field. I understood this when I talked with my sisters and sister-in-law about the ups and downs of such a lonely, codependent existence. We were holding on to a single basket of apples while complaining about the monotony of fruit. Three years later, a neighbor informed me she'd had no idea that my mother was an athlete—a long-distance runner and an endurance champion. It seemed my niece would spend all her days following her grandmother around, and at night would fall asleep clinging to my mother's stinky feet. When she got to school age and had to leave for the day, they would walk hand in hand to the village green before parting. The onset of elementary school made this separation inevitable and necessary. But then the day came when my niece got back from school and my mother thought her head felt a little hot, uncomfortably so, and rushed her inside, where she laid a cool towel soaked in well water on her forehead. My mother then went off to cook, but when she came back, she found her granddaughter asleep on the floor, the towel by her side like an outstretched arm. In a panic, she darted over and put her hand to the girl's head.

The heat radiating from her forehead shocked my mother like an electric current, jolting her hand away. "Yuanyuan! Yuanyuan!" she yelled and shook her. Her feverish, stricken body was limp as a willow branch, as a cooked noodle, and slumped this way and that without waking. In an absolute frenzy, my mother scooped up her granddaughter and dashed through the town toward the hospital. This might be the only time in her life she'd flat-out sprinted. Passersby gawked at her speeding legs. Buildings, trees, and telegraph poles flashed by, and she left them all in her wake. "What's wrong?" people called. "What happened?" Her only answer was to keep running, all the way from our home down the main road, through the center of town to the bus station. There, about halfway to the hospital, my cousin Changke caught up with her and took the girl like the baton in a relay race. He ran the rest of the way to the hospital, which was just outside town.

Yuanyuan had a fever of forty-one degrees. The doctor said we were lucky that our home wasn't too far from the hospital. If we were deeper in the countryside, four or five kilometers away, the fever might have burned up every vestige of life, or turned into meningitis that would have left her deaf or witless. Luckily, we did live nearby, and my mother had the speed and endurance of a long-distance runner. Having reached the hospital, my mother slumped to the ground, sweating through her clothes and panting urgently like an aged cow dragging along a sickly calf and broken cart, trudging toward the peak of her life, although she was actually already past the peak. My niece woke up with a drip in her arm and smiled as she called out, "Grandma …"

Mother answered with a smile and took her hand. In that moment, they fully understood the beauty of being completely dependent on another person, the warmest possible glow. The following year, I got promoted, and from then on I sent my mother as much money as I could each month. When for some reason I skipped a couple of months, I got a letter from my niece. The writing on the white envelope was lopsided as wind-blown branches, swaying this way and that. The eight-cent stamp glared at me like a peculiar eye.

I opened the letter and was confronted by a single line:

Uncle, my grandma says she's run out of money.

Nothing else. The shortest message I've ever received, out of tens of thousands of letters and emails, and also the most meaningful and emotionally resonant. In that one line I could see my mother and niece in the old courtyard, in the isolated village, their quiet harmony, the sturdiness and depth of that eternal relationship that was part of the natural order of things. I saw the endless glory and simplicity of our home, our hometown, that patch of earth. Thank God I was born into this family, onto this piece of land, that I had such parents, such siblings, such in-laws, such cousins. When the war with Vietnam was at its most explosive and soldiers weren't allowed to write home, I got another letter from my niece that my mother had told her to send. This one contained not a single word, just a dozen red and blue stamps. For a long time, I had no idea what my mother was trying to tell me. When I was finally able to go home, I asked and she said, "If you're busy and don't have time to write, just stick a stamp on an empty envelope and send it, so at least I'll know you're okay."

At the time of this conversation, my mother, my niece, and I were standing in our courtyard in late autumn, beneath a crystalline sky with thin clouds wafting across it like white silk threads, exquisite as black words on white paper in an annal. The sky was so vast, borderless, and expansive, and it felt as tender as my niece's tiny hand within mine.

Manual Labor and Women's Life Studies

1.

Everyone in a village was a laborer.

The word "labor" had a particular valence here. For instance, it was always connected to the soil and the earth; to hard work and revolution; to men and power. When we said someone was a laborer, it tended to be a masculine form of praise. We seldom referred to a woman in this way, unless she was designated a "model laborer" in China's collective production, in which case we would publicly refer to her by this title.

"Laborer" is the lowliest form of pride in a man. In order to maintain this gender separation, we referred to women who did manual labor as "workers." Witness the breadth and capacity of the Chinese language. A woman's "work" encompassed more than toiling in the fields as hard as the men; when she got back home, an endless list of chores awaited her: cooking, laundry, mending, child care. After she'd made a meal, she was responsible for serving it to the old folks, her husband, her children. When they were done eating, she'd wash every bowl, every dish, and put it back in its place in the kitchen. If her children didn't have clothes to wear, that was another knock on womanhood—all wives, all mothers. If the house was dirty, if there were dust and clutter on the floor, the woman would have to pay for it—the wife, the mother.

Not calling women's labor "labor" but "work" expands the category to an even greater number of tasks, an even greater ordeal than mere labor.

2.

My mother was a fairly typical worker in our village.

As I recall, when it came time for the production brigade to plow deep into the earth, she'd go down to the fields with the men. When a canal needed maintenance, she'd be in there heaving rocks out of the water alongside the men. At harvest time, she naturally got up in the middle of the night and worked till the cruel sun was high overhead, pulling the stone roller with everyone else, like a team of oxen, to grind the wheat grains. In the growing season, when the men were free to lounge around sunning themselves and rolling cigarettes, she—like almost all the women in the village, the wives and mothers—was expected to remain in her courtyard or doorstep with her sewing kit, reinforcing cloth shoes, mending garments, or sewing on missing buttons, for her husbands and four kids.

In those days, the insecticide used in farming villages was known as six-six powder, a reddish-yellow substance. My mother would use a towel as a makeshift mask across her mouth and nose, and sprinkle the stuff over the fields and crops whenever they got infested. A day or two later, her palms would swell and her fingers would thicken to the size of plastic pipes. If anyone touched them, the skin would split with a cracking sound and bloody liquid would gush out. Her face would be swollen too, red and shiny, and she would scream in pain, "Mama!" at the slightest contact. Eventually, progress arrived and the village acquired gloves and masks, but by then six-six powder had been replaced by DDT, and when that was sprayed on our cotton bushes, fruit trees, or vegetable fields, not only did it cause face and hand swelling, even legs encased in long trousers would grow elephantine, as bad as during the three years of famine. Mother and the other young women in the village would sit around the village green, gazing at the fields and sky, and grumble, "It was better before we had progress. This pesticide isn't just killing pests, it's killing people too!"

Then society progressed even further, and DDT became the default solution to exterminate all kinds of vermin. Mother and the other women her age passed this work on to their daughters and the young women who married into our village. They—the mothers—went around lamenting, "Why can't I see clearly?" "How come my fingers can't bend anymore?" "As soon as I take a few steps, my knees start hurting." They were only in their forties but had eyesight as bad as any old person's. When any of them wanted to thread a needle, she had to go outside in search of better light, or else entreat one of her children or some other young person to guide the thread into the eye, just as the thread of her life was sliding into decrepitude.

I was in my teens when my mother began prematurely ageing. After her eyes started blurring, she was always sticking slivers of ginger into them, so the spiciness would make her tear up and temporarily brighten them. If we had no ginger at home, she'd peel a strip or two from a scallion. If we were out of onions, shreds of chili. Luckily we were sufficiently well-off to almost always have ginger or scallions on hand. She'd stick ginger into her eyes in the spring, all the way to autumn, then winter would be upon us, when everyone else could take a break but she got even busier. Because my mother was skilled at making clothes and we had a secondhand sewing machine from Luoyang city, our neighbors and other villagers would come round with bolts of cloth, with a blushing bride- or groom-to-be in tow who'd shyly stand before my mother to be measured with a ruler. She'd scrawl the numbers on the cloth, then line the rolls of fabric up in order on our table. I watched as my mother worked nonstop, cutting the cloth to size, sitting at the machine and working the treadle, constantly grabbing the bright yellow piece of ginger from the table and scraping off a couple of shreds with her fingernail, tilted her head back and dropping them into her eyes, then rubbing with both hands. When she finally lowered her hands, they'd be streaked with tears. She'd dry them on her trousers, and the clattering of the machine would start up again.

Like a poet scribbling away, my mother composed an ongoing saga of countryside life on her sewing machine, encompassing the lives and tales of village women like herself. Clouds scudded across the sky, the river babbled, and our days moved inexorably through murky confusion. Her sons and daughters grew up in this muddled rural ode. The soil grew exhausted in her verses. Her children and other young locals got married, and now there were even more people calling her auntie, mother, grandma. Clouds rose and faded away, the sun descended behind the western hills. She couldn't pinpoint exactly when this began, but all kinds of illnesses were spreading through her, like roads leading in all directions from the village. Many believe that roads are formed by people walking, but almost every road was there long before your birth, laid out across the great land, waiting for you to walk down this one or that. In the end, some places have no roads, and only intrepid explorers can forge a path through. As for us—my mother, father, sisters, brother, and sister-in-law, and those around us—we were born to walk down other people's roads, to take lives that had already been lived and live them once again, and then again.

My mother spent her whole existence repeating other people's lives, just as we are all treading in our parents' footsteps. Other women—women and men, really—in village fields and courtyards are constantly busy, industriously toiling away, and before they know it, they get old and weak. Like everyone else, like all the women in the village, my mother worked industriously, and somehow her forties became her fifties, then her sixties. Other people got sick for no reason, and so did she. Some people like my eldest sister became familiar at a young age with the pharmacy and hospital and doctors—you'd have thought they were her neighbors, the very best people. My mother was on intimate terms with them from a young age too. Every two or three days she'd drop by to get something off her chest. The road to the hospital was as familiar as the way to the wheat fields, vegetable garden, or her own kitchen. At first, she went because her back and legs hurt, and she revered painkillers the way true believers venerate churches and their god. Then later, she went for small procedures here and there, pain and bloodletting, needles going into her as if she were one of her garments.

No one could tell us why, but my mother's body was covered in lumps of fatty tissue, maybe twenty or thirty of them, on her legs, arms, back, and torso. First they were the size of beans, then over time they grew to be as large as peach stones, then dates, then walnuts, purple-green bumps under her skin, neither painful nor itchy, like one burden after another on the body of history, out of mind until you remember they exist. But when these things appear on a joint, like a knee or wrist or elbow, they hurt as they grow. A little ache, then a sharper pain. Soon you'll need surgery if you want to keep your mobility. Then you have no choice. You need to get cut open, bleed, and be sewn up again. We ended up on the road from our village to the hospital and the operating room, leaving behind my mother's footprints like fallen leaves in the autumn. The main issue was that these bumps loved appearing on her joints, just as the protuberances and scars of China's history are inevitably located at its turning points.

My mother didn't just have a few surgical scars. If I said she had eight or ten, that would be an underestimate. When she was fifty, after a handful of these little procedures, we brought her to the army hospital in Kaifeng to have a tumor on her uterus removed. I happened to be a clerk at the hospital then, and as the poet says, "the pavilion by the water gets the moonlight first."[3] As a family member, she got priority treatment. In the six hours she was under, they removed many of these bumps, ranging in size from a grape to a steamed bun. Afterward, the army doctor stared uncomprehendingly at the dozen or so excised growths in his tray and said, "Countryside women can sure put up with a lot!"

I wasn't sure if he was trying to commend or make fun of me. All I know is that in and around my village, there aren't just a handful of women like my mother, but dozens, no, hundreds, maybe more than a thousand. Tradition has made each of them believe that her existence, revolving as it does around housework and labor, is simply her destiny, that being born a woman means taking on "men's work" without relinquishing any of their existing "women's work." Hence premature aging. Hence early-onset illness. So many more women's footsteps than men's on the pathways and roads to our village clinics, to the hospital in town, and in the county seat, to the bigger ones in Luoyang and Zhengzhou. All of this is an inescapable aspect of rural women's lives, and a completely neglected part of "the female question."

3.

I ought to say that my mother is one of the more fortunate people in my village.

It wasn't just that after I was promoted in the army, I was able to send her a monthly allowance. Nor that after I became an author—a "famous" author—the county chief and party secretary, along with the other cadres in town, were anxious to take very good care of "Lianke's mother" in all kinds of ways. Most importantly, after I'd become a resident of Beijing, she could come to the capital for all her medical treatments—even if they were misdiagnosed.

The head of the county hospital was my good friend, and according to his analysis, rural women were far more likely to be hospitalized than men, by a ratio of around 3:2. An interesting medical conundrum: Why do middle-aged and older rural women get ill at a much higher rate than men, yet still have a longer life span? The science may not account for the fact that women face harsher conditions with far more adaptability and fortitude than men. That's an unshakable truth.

At one point, my mother had knee replacement surgery, and once again she demonstrated such endurance and understanding of life, existence, and work that to this day I feel she was giving me a lesson in "women's life studies." This was over a decade ago, when she was seventy-two, and the pain in her knee finally got so bad that she couldn't walk. My brother, sister-in-law, and I decided to get her admitted into a Beijing hospital, where she could get a new kneecap fitted. I asked around and pulled a few strings to get her a place, an inescapable part of China's medical system. The problem came a day or two after the operation, when the very cordial doctor insisted that the patient had to move around so the imported, man-made patella could get in sync with the natural one. And so, oozing sweat and shedding tears, my mother walked down a Chinese road with her German-made kneecap, leaning against walls and dragging herself along, one difficult step after another. A week later, according to the doctor's instructions, she was supposed to lie down and have someone press slowly on her bent knee for half an hour or so, and the resultant agony made her life feel even worse than death. When my brother pushed down, she screeched and begged him to stop. She sounded like she was kneeling before him, pleading for mercy.

He did as she asked, but after she'd wiped away her tears and sweat, she abruptly asked, "Why did you stop?"

"You told me to."

"No matter what I say, you have to keep pushing. What if

you stop and I can't walk after that? I'd have gone through that surgery for nothing!"

So he pressed down hard on the artificial kneecap, and she sobbed and pleaded with him to be gentle, to spare her knee and her life. She would rather die than suffer like this, she screamed. When he stopped again, she dried her face and said, "Do as the doctor told you. Press down for as long as he said. You can't quit just because I asked you to."

He started again, and she started screaming, but this time he persisted, turning aside so he wouldn't have to look at her contorted face. When the time was finally up, she'd exhausted herself and shredded her throat with shrieking. My brother stopped, washed his hands and tear-streaked face, and left. When he was gone, my mother said a few things to me about life, existence, and feminism.

"Your brother was so harsh with me," she said. "As if I'm not his mother."

I laughed. "It's *because* you're his mother that he can be so forceful."

She thought about it. "Obviously, women suffer much more than men. Your dad went so early, and left all the suffering for me."

I pondered that. "You shouldn't say that. This operation cost over sixty grand. Over eighty grand including the hospital stay. Back in the day, we only had one or two thousand to our names. Anyway, Dad didn't die *that* young."

She stared at me for a very long time. "Did it really cost eighty thousand?"

I nodded.

"If we spent that much, you should tell your brother to press harder next time. Otherwise, we might as well have dropped all that money into the river."

And so, a week later, no matter how hard my brother pushed, my mother didn't utter a sound, not even when her tears and sweat had soaked her pillow. She was quiet at the half-month mark too, still weeping and sweating, and she could climb stairs on her own now. One month in, not only could she walk and climb stairs unaided, when it came time for her to be discharged and head home, she insisted on carrying her own suitcase as she boarded the train. "I need the practice, otherwise we'll have wasted our money. A person who can't walk is no different from a dead person." After getting home, she'd stroll round the village green and along the river each morning, then in the evening she'd gather the other women and old folk, and my sister would put on some music and lead them in calisthenics. All these ideas, subjects, and philosophies—daily existence, life itself, womanhood—along with feminism, played out in the village with a mingling of sadness and joy, working in harmony, like a windmill singing as the west wind blows, grains of sand applauding the yellow earth as a breeze stirs. We could draw a clear line between the study of men and women, between men's and women's rights, but this separation is undone because everyone is scrabbling to survive, to exist, and like milk and water blending, everything is intermingled. Labor and work, life and existence and destiny, all thrown into the same pot and turned into stew, which then gets served on the great square of humanity.

New Year Scrub

When my mother was eighty, I gave her a scrub.

This sort of thing, bathing and foot washing and fingernail trimming, had previously been done for her by my sisters, brother, and sister-in-law. But then a few years ago, she spent New Year's in Beijing. We had a family tradition of getting thoroughly cleansed to start the year, which we followed like it was the law. On the last night of the lunar calendar, in the unnatural quiet because of Beijing's prohibition of firecrackers, we turned on every overhead light, standing lamp, and wall light in the apartment, until the entire place was bright as day, trying to manufacture some of the bustle and fantasy of New Year. Amid all this festivity, my mother's turn for a bath came. My wife turned on the bathroom lights and started the hot water running, and when the room was nice and warm, my mother told my wife she could go.

My wife came out and said, smiling tenderly, "Our ma doesn't want me to see her get undressed." I was watching TV with my son and daughter-in-law, and at my wife's words we all burst out laughing, and in that instant we felt a blast of warmth as if a winter firepit had banished the icy Beijing cold. We nibbled on melon seeds, peanuts, candies, and chocolates, watching TV and listening to the splashing from the bathroom. After a while, my wife pushed open the door and asked my mother if she wanted a backrub. My mother said, "No need, it's fine." A while later, my daughter-in-law pushed the door and asked the same question, and got the same answer. She too smiled and retreated. A few minutes went by, and my son asked once more through the door. Amid more splashing sounds, she said she was fine, she could handle it on her own.

Yet for some reason, the whole family felt we ought to help my mother scrub her back. On the living room sofa, we glanced at the clock, then the TV. My mother rarely spent more than half an hour in the bath, and if we didn't get this done soon, we'd lose our chance. This caused a mild stirring of panic, and I realized everyone was looking at me.

I moved my one-year-old granddaughter from my lap to the couch, and like my wife, son, and daughter-in-law before me, I went to the bathroom door, opened it a crack, and said, "How about a little scrub? Get your skin squeaky clean and it won't itch."

My mother stuck her head past the glass barrier and said, "Come in, then."

And so I gained permission to enter.

Four lights blazed overhead, and the room was thick with water droplets, steam and fog, like a rainbow or clouds after a storm, color and beauty wafting through the air. Amid this moist radiance, I saw my mother's dirty clothes in a heap on the floor, and her clean ones hanging from the wall. She was behind the glass like an ancient bodhisattva, between light and water. In that moment, she wasn't female or a woman to me; I thought only that she was my mother. Just as I wasn't male or a man to her, all she knew was that I was her son. And so, after we'd exchanged a look, I opened the partition and she handed me the washcloth in her hand. It felt completely natural to rub her back, her shoulders, her neck. Then she turned around to face me, and I did the same on her arms, wrists, and hands.

Looking at the nude body of my eighty-year-old mother in the bath, I felt like a true believer gazing at the holy mother. She was in a pair of shorts, sodden and clinging to her body, and nothing else, bare and gleaming in the light, her chest, her back, her pendulous bosom, her sagging belly (how ugly it was), and those mottled fatty lumps here and there.

So this is what my mother had become.

Short, fat, and hideous, with straggly white hair and a double chin, breasts like drooping hemp sacks, like time itself and the history of women hanging cumbersomely from her body. I sloughed the debris from her back and arms, gray as extraneous memories shed from the corpus of history. Bit by bit I scraped her clean, and she let me, like a child. When I was done, up and down, back and front, she did everywhere else, the parts she could easily reach, and I handed her a towel.

"Did that feel nice?"

She smiled. "I'm grotesque. When we get old, we barely look human."

"So what?" I smiled back. "It happens to everyone in the end."

We exchanged another look, and I went out. Shutting the door behind me, I mopped the sweat off my face and noticed the rest of the family watching me with bright, envious smiles, as if I'd been given a special award none of them had. But it also felt like all of us had just eaten the most delicious Belgian chocolates.

New Year's Eve in Beijing is the same kind of cold as deep autumn, but in our home, on that night, it felt like noontime in the middle of spring. We huddled together, waiting. When the bathroom door creaked open, my wife and daughter-in-law went over to help her to the sofa, while my son and I stood and waited for her. Those few steps, those few seconds, were like the sacred mother or an aged bodhisattva approaching us. My son grinned at his grandmother. "How do you feel? Was that good?" Before she could answer, I said to my son, "Your grandma is so fair, her skin is pale as milk." My mother blushed and smiled as she elegantly summed up the entirety of a woman's life and age. "I'm so ugly. I've lived my whole life within this ugliness."

My God. What a profound statement.

6
The Third Sex—Female Otherness

Interlude 9

1.

So, please don't read what follows like it's some kind of thesis.

All of this is just idle musing. If you don't like what it says, feel free to skip ahead to Chapter 7. Maybe that will bring you the same pleasure as overtaking another car.

The iconic Simone de Beauvoir isn't famous because of her novels, nor for her Goncourt-winning *The Mandarins*, but because she boldly proclaimed, making her mark on history and humanity, "One is not born, but rather becomes, woman."[1] *The Second Sex* was published in 1949 and swept through France, Europe, the US, and then the world, capturing the attention of anyone interested in the contemporary condition of women, and cementing the establishment of feminist studies. Through scholarly knowledge and personal experience, as well as mountains of historical, literary, and anecdotal evidence, Beauvoir proved that women are not born into their gender but rather sculpted and assembled into it by society. This framework and way of thinking resonated with many, and shaped the way individuals, communities, and legal systems accorded respect and dignity to women. During the lengthy debates and liberation movements that followed, it seemed this question kept sliding into the theoretical battle of "a woman isn't a womb" versus "a woman is a womb," all the way until the 1970s, when titans of the feminist movement such as Simone Veil and Antoinette Fouque broke the stalemate and brought the fight to all corners of society. Fouque's *There Are Two Sexes* spoke from the point of view of the female libido, using psychological and political analysis to conclude that the female desire for reproduction is a primeval, fundamental source of creation, like the need for sunlight in the cold or the hunger for food. She boldly proclaimed this to be uterine desire: "I was born a girl and reborn a woman after giving birth to a girl. Thus despite the oppression of all the symbolic institutions (reinforced by the *diktat* of a certain feminism), I assumed the psychophysiological destiny of my sex."[2] We see a contradiction between Beauvoir's and Fouque's points of view. In Fouque's many writings, she critiqued and mocked Beauvoir's "misogyny." Fouque believed she was born female, a view Beauvoir rejected. Beauvoir wrote of women,

> Their lot is one with that of perishable things; they would lose everything in losing them. Only a free subject, asserting himself beyond time, can foil destruction; this supreme recourse is forbidden to the woman. It is mainly because she has never experienced the powers of liberty that she does not believe in liberation; the

> world to her seems governed by an obscure destiny against which it is presumptuous to react.[3]

(How like a manifesto this sounds.) "A woman is shut up in a kitchen or a boudoir, and one is surprised her horizon is limited; her wings are cut, and then she is blamed for not knowing how to fly."[4] Whether we look at feminism or women's studies, they are a fraught battlefield of ideas and discoveries pitting nature against nurture. Fouque, saying she was born a girl who then "assumed the psychophysiological destiny of [her] sex," describes her journey from the inborn to the learned in her life and nature, whereas Beauvoir's "One is not born, but rather becomes, woman" takes the path of politics, society, and culture to a much greater and more complicated arena. *The Second Sex* posits opposition to maleness but also suggests that those born female take on a "second sex" at a later point in their lives. Fouque's assertion that "there are two sexes" points first and foremost to the male-female binary, and secondarily to a "second sex" apart from the femaleness that stands in opposition to maleness. At this juncture, my idle speculation is that there is a "new category of womanhood" in between the other two—a femaleness between male and female that is separate from the female.

2.

The new category is the otherness of the female.

The otherness of the female is a sort of wart on womankind.

Whether a wart is inborn or developed later in life, it is a useless, meaningless growth, but when you try to remove it, there will be much bleeding and possible side effects, making you think it might have been better to leave it intact. Yet if you do, as the days and months accumulate, once you have coexisted for a long time with your wart, you may no longer find it extraneous but rather a part of your physiology and life. A family member, a personal possession. A responsibility or mission that you must live up to and pass on. (My God.)

In *The Second Sex*, Beauvoir declares right at the outset of the chapter "Childhood":

> One is not born, but rather becomes, woman. No biological, psychic, or economic destiny defines the figure that the human female takes on in society; it is civilization as a whole that elaborates this intermediary product between the male and the eunuch that is called feminine …
>
> On the contrary, for the woman there is, from the start, a conflict between her autonomous existence and her "beingother"; she is taught that to please, she must try to please, must make herself object; she must therefore renounce her autonomy. She is treated like a living doll, and freedom is denied her; thus a vicious circle is closed; for the less she exercises her freedom to understand, grasp, and discover the world around her, the less she will find its resources, and the less she will dare to affirm herself as subject.[5]

This (very serious) discourse from *The Second Sex* talks about what those who "become … woman" must accept and permit during this becoming. When I talk (recklessly, wildly) about "the new category," I firstly mean to transcend these things that women have been taught to put up with since childhood. Girls encounter the coming of their period with surprise and terror, and having accepted this inborn phenomenon, they gradually also take on the idea that women "must" do the sewing and cooking and bearing of children, the burden of the second sex, her responsibilities and circumstances. Other than that, in my hometown, on that piece of earth, apart from her first sex of the life and physiology (femaleness) she is born with, a girl will also "become … woman" (in Beauvoir's formulation) through the forces of history and politics, but there is also the new category given to her by our history, environment, and culture. A woman is inherent femaleness, plus the second sex brought by historical and political forces, then in that vast wilderness, our culture, circumstances, and shared past insist that she must take on certain characteristics understood to be male, a novel category: an otherness forced upon women by the imposition of another identity, that of a "worker for socialism."

3.

Amid this exultation, none of the notable feminists and thinkers—neither Simone de Beauvoir nor Simone Veil of France, ground zero of European feminism and women's studies, nor Antoinette Fouque, nor Susan Bordo nor Judith Butler from the US, where feminism is still in the ascendant and where it has a material rather than philosophical tendency—have disputed the fundamental reality that human beings tend to be born into two genders. We respect the equality and freedom of these genders and their differences, just as we recognize that an elm tree is an elm tree, and a paulownia is a paulownia. Nonetheless, at particular times and places, elms and paulownias might get lumped together as "northern trees," denatured and politicized or historicized, removed from the realm of culture and the spirit.

Not only is Mao Zedong's "women hold up half the sky" a universally known slogan in China, it has also garnered much acclaim in the heated debate over women's issues across the world (in which we take much pride). According to Fouque, "Mao Tse-Tung's famous line, 'Women hold up the other half of the sky,' is unquestionably one of the sources, the most poetical one, of the Women's Liberation Movement in France."[6] In 1965, those who took to the streets to protest and spread the word of this movement in France were all familiar with the words of this great Asian. They were encouraged and motivated by these words, and they celebrated and rejoiced for China's women (womankind). The strange thing is, to this day, no one in China knows when or where exactly this great feminist quote was said. Scholars have pored over the archives and records and found no trace of Chairman Mao's speaking these words. No one can prove that he uttered them in the first place. Still, in 1965, Mao went for a swim—one of his favorite activities—at the Ming Tombs Reservoir outside Beijing and afterward had a historically significant talk with some young people. During this conversation, he said, "Times have changed. Men and women are the same now. Anything a male comrade can do, a female comrade can do too." Which goes to show that the chairman took a liberal, enlightened approach to "women's issues." This legacy of female emancipation and equality still endures today, a strong support from which the flag of "women's rights" continues to fly. However, we cannot overlook that the Ming Tombs Reservoir was built in 1958 during the Great Leap Forward (such a distinctive era), and during this turbulent time, this medium-sized reservoir was completely built with the most primitive methods, heavy loads carried on the shoulder or by hand by hundreds of thousands of laborers, to a plan personally organized and overseen by Zhou Enlai. The whole thing took over five months from beginning to end, over 160 days. Amid the festivities for this much-lauded public works project of the Great Leap Forward, many national heroines emerged, such as the "seven sisters" or the "nine Lan group," who subsequently had movies made about them and were sent abroad for press events and to study. This goes back to 1955, when agricultural production was at its height, and a farming cooperative was set up in Yanglongsi's Baozi village, Xifeng county, Guizhou province. The men earned 7 work points for a day of labor, while the women only got 2.5 work points. As a result, almost all the women refused to go into the fields, which led to a labor shortage so severe that the community wasn't able to feed itself, leaving them with no choice but to increase the women's compensation. That year, a (groundbreaking and excellent) essay titled "Bringing About Equal Compensation for Men and Women in Cooperatives" was published in the magazine of the Guizhou Women's Federation, and Chairman Mao praised it while suggesting that "all villages and cooperatives should follow suit." As a result, pay parity became not just a guiding principle of women's liberation in China but also a practical measure that was put into place. Despite the unknown origins of the quote "women hold up half the sky," it resonated through the world with the force of truth. Even Fouque was excited and uplifted by it. Yet within China, anyone who's been paying attention knows that the fundamental meaning of these words is intimately entwined with the concepts of labor, work, the Great Leap Forward, and socialism. Without the need for huge quantities of labor during the Great Leap Forward and the establishment of socialist society, this quote and the discourse around it might never have arisen, and in turn the transformation of the treatment and acknowledgment of women across all levels and areas of Chinese society, which elevated their position and gave them the right to work outside the home, might never have happened. At the very least, this slogan freed women from the courtyard, the home, and the kitchen, allowing them to stand between the sun and rain, on the work floor of the Great Leap Forward and in the farming fields afterward.

Is this not a good thing? It's very good.

As with cutting off men's queues and unbinding women's feet during the Republican era, this was a magnificent, historic marker of progress, a significant milestone in social anthropology and feminism. Yet if we were to expand the scope of our inquiry, in the spirit of "women hold up half the sky" and "times have changed, men and women are alike now," to the fields of politics, culture, finance, education, and government administration, where labor is not needed in the same way, we would find that women's liberation played out differently than in the farming fields or factories: "Anything a male comrade can do, a female comrade can do too." Outside of these work arenas, women haven't been accorded true freedom or equality, nor have their rights or humanity truly been respected. In these bastions of patriarchy, the sneering, dismissive attitude of "Ugh, women—heh heh" still prevails. If we only see women holding up half the sky at times when the nation and the era most need labor and sweaty exertion, how can we imagine the ideals and principles of feminism such as freedom, equality, and equal rights? How can we keep conquest, exploitation, occupation, prejudices, ulterior motives, and so on from lurking underneath these lofty words?

During the Great Leap Forward, under the banner of "women hold up half the sky," the Luhun Reservoir was built a few kilometers from our home, on an even bigger, more ambitious scale than the Ming Tombs Reservoir. This was before the Three Gorges or Xiaolangdi Dams; at the time, the Luhun Reservoir was the ninth largest in China. You can imagine the magnificent scene: rural folk mobilized by the thousands, building a reservoir with only the most primitive tools. After this high point, when the lights had gone down and the curtain of history descended, reducing the performers onstage to mere spectators of the times, my mother would often think back to the moment when she and almost all the able-bodied women from miles around were called upon to move rocks, dredge basketfuls of mud, smash boulders and carry sand, and she would say with feeling, "We were all crazy back then. People weren't treated as humans. We worked for more than ten hours every day, for a few months on end, maybe more than half a year. We got so exhausted, we'd collapse on the ground and fall asleep with our harnesses still on." Whenever she spoke about how women were "liberated" to go work on the dam, a peculiar, uncomprehending smile would appear on her face, then she'd mumble, "Women weren't treated as women either. We weren't allowed to take even half a day off when our period came. Some of us had to carry sand and break rocks with blood streaming down our trousers onto the ground."

My mother's experience is a commonplace one, just another example of what women went through after the founding of the New China in 1949, during the establishment of socialism before the era of reform and opening up. There's nothing unique about her situation, but by recognizing and articulating that "women weren't treated as women," she has unintentionally turned herself into an emblem of the village woman and a feminist, plain and simple. This is the complex, inescapable issue of logic, philosophy, and women's studies: that a woman is also a person, and as a person, is still a woman. Then, with the simplicity, materiality, and labor of her existence, she makes clear that a woman is a person but not a man—and yet, she has no choice but to take on some of the traditional attributes of a man. A position only a Chinese woman could fully inhabit. A third category.

4.

When talking about the otherness of women—the new category—I can't help thinking of my mother, my sisters, and all the other women I know from our village. What does it mean to be a woman in the Chinese countryside? This has nothing to do with sexual orientation, or the homosexuality or bisexuality that is a frequent topic within feminism.

It feels as if these ideas have nothing to do with the women, the womenfolk, from our village.

Even so, I believe women who live on this piece of earth almost all have a sort of "manliness." Hybrids of history and politics. A rugged energy that we could term the otherness of womanhood, a masculinity conferred upon them by their lives, cultures, dispositions, and environments, and particularly by the times they live in, their nation, and ideologies. In other words, they take on the roles that women "ought to" take on: pregnancy, childbirth, raising children, and the many varied tasks of running a household. To an extent, they are then also compelled to accept a "man's" duties and responsibilities: planting, tilling, fertilizing, harvesting, and so on. Things that almost all men do. For millennia, women have been shackled to the principle of "women indoors, men outdoors." After these restraints were smashed in 1949, women did not see their burdens lifted—rather, they were expected to take on a significant share of men's tasks too. Now they were working both indoors and outdoors, doing both men's and women's work. Once again they were controlled and exploited, sacrificing and working twice as much as before.

The men didn't seem to be putting in any less effort, yet the women were clearly taking on a much greater share of the responsibilities, duties, and labor. Where was all this extra work going? To the "construction of socialism" that took place after 1949. Before this, China's rural villages were essentially self-governing, with each household running according to its needs. Society was structured with women running the home and men working in the fields. After 1949, this loose, easy equilibrium of small units was forcibly bound together and absorbed into the larger entities of people's communes. The structure of each household stayed the same, but outside the home, the territorial expansion of socialism was relentless; there were only so many acres of farmland, but the speed of this growth meant that working from dawn till dusk was no longer sufficient, and apart from the expanses of the crop fields, there were also waterways and steelworks, and the imperative to "catch up with Britain and overtake America," which increased the scope of labor into the mountains and forests, the seas and rivers. Motivated by ideology and propelled by power, the demand for labor spread like an endlessly expanding battlefield. The burden on men increased, and even then, more workers were needed. Women had to fill the gap.

While going through Fouque's *There Are Two Sexes*, which felt like reading a most unusual novel, I came upon an astounding set of statistics: "Whereas women produce two-thirds of global wealth, they own only 1 percent of it, get a mere 10 percent of disposable income, and constitute 75 percent of the world's poorest inhabitants."[7] (For more information, see the 2012 analysis by the UN Development Programme, UN Population Fund, and World Health Organization.) I can't help thinking of our great undertaking in establishing socialism. What if our country's resources were distributed along similar lines, that is to say, two-thirds of wealth being created by women even though they only got to own 1 percent of it and earn 10 percent of disposable income? This puts me in mind of my mother, my sisters, and all the other women on our piece of earth. Taking the busiest season of the year, wheat harvest, as a basis for calculation: In planting season, women toil like oxen, pulling seed distributors along with ropes; when the wheat sprouts, they hoe and weed alongside the men; while fertilizing, the men carry baskets of dung back and forth along the road between the village and the fields, and the women do exactly the same, with baskets that are every bit as large as the men's. In this arid northern climate, the men must water the fields in the middle of the night, and the women are right there too. When the wheat is golden, scythes are sharpened, then the wheat is reaped, bundled, threshed, dried, and stored, and in all of this toil, women put in just as much work as men, sometimes even more, yet in the songs and odes that celebrate the harvest, paeans to "the owners of the land" and labor, it's only the men who are extolled. Even now, can we truly say that the achievements of men and women are equally split? That he puts in 50 percent of the work, and so does she? Even if this calculation stands, with all the tasks that this season brings, even at the busiest times, it is still women who prepare three meals a day and have to serve them to the men as they lounge in the shade of a tree; women must do the washing up, laundry, and yardwork while men smoke and chat idly; women sew and mend for their husbands and children, and line their shoes. All these many, many chores that take up so much time and energy are unequivocally taken on by women. If we count them as a part of women's labor—and there's no reason why we shouldn't—alongside shouldering half the farming work, then it's clear that women are putting in far more work than men are. Taking a step back, if we consider the planting of crops, the raising of livestock, and the building of waterworks in rural villages to be part of our country's (and socialism's) accomplishments, then women's housework should be included here too. Just as no war can be won if logistics are neglected, and therefore we have to consider logistics and supply lines to be part of warfare—arguably the most crucial part that decides whether a war will be won or lost, in the same vein, if we include the many, many domestic chores as part of the history and labor of nation-building, then what reason can we have to say that women have contributed any less than men, who make such a fuss over their planting and harvesting, the dams and roads and bridges they build?

I don't doubt the findings and analysis of the UN and WHO. Women produce two-thirds of global wealth but only own 1 percent of it. I think of my mother in the sixties, in the midst of nation-building, when she worked with such enthusiasm that she was proclaimed a model laborer of her commune and her brigade, earning red and yellow certificates and citations. She used to have these up on the walls of our home, but at some point she quietly put them all away. When I asked her why, she smiled simply and said something both vague and highly enlightened, "How embarrassing. I've never felt women ought to compete with men for these things."

I don't know where her awards are now, but they vanished without a trace. With them no longer on display, a span of history has grown blurry, as has the role of women within this stretch of the past. Simply gone. Like a play that has gone from A to B, from the past to now, and along the way, the actors in one or more roles have been quietly swapped out.

5.

After my mother got shy about her awards and made them go away, the magnificent moment of nation-building shifted within my family from the past to the present. The great era of reform and opening up arrived. As age forced my mother to withdraw from the stage, my sisters and sister-in-law, as well as my niece and great-nieces, were all ushered into this glorious period as they began their lives and careers. The wheels turned, and life flowed on. When the focus of reform and opening up moved to the cities, rural villages were no longer key sites of this transformation, but rather turned into warehouses providing an inexhaustible supply of workers to be delivered to the city, and the otherness of women, the incursion of the new category, became even more subtle, individual, and cruel. When our home, our village, our piece of land, and almost all men and women were labeled "rural workers" and surged into the factories, workshops, construction sites, street corners, production lines, and domestic homes of the cities, everyone realized that in two completely different eras, the otherness of women workers remained the same, except in the earlier time, women's otherness was forced upon them by history. At that time, if a woman were to say: "I'm a woman, I can't work in the fields alongside men during the period of land reform and cooperatives; I can't cut down trees and forge steel alongside men during the Great Leap Forward; I can't haul sand and carry rocks alongside men during the era of dam-building"—if you said any of those things, you'd be hauled on stage to be publicly denounced in a struggle session and get paraded through the streets. Thousands of people would laugh at you. You wouldn't be human; you wouldn't even be a woman. But now, in this great era of reform and opening up, the hand of history has been hidden, and no one seems to be holding the syringe to forcibly inject the mores of the times into women's bodies. But the market, money, and desire, which appear to exist freely within the reality and spirit of society and culture, through some formless hand and shapeless strength, induce women themselves to pick up this syringe and shoot it into their own veins.

I have passed many times through "Henan Village" in Beijing's Changping neighborhood and walked through Beijing's many markets, interviewing the Henan people who collect trash and operate elevators, especially the women among them, to ask if they had no choice but to come here to work. They all said they didn't *have* to, but if you're "living for others," what choice did you have except to leave home in search of work?

My second sister encouraged her children to seek work in the faraway South and offered to bring up her grandchild so her daughter-in-law could work and earn more money. At certain times of year, such as in August when the cotton flowers bloom in Xinjiang, and the sun rains fire down on the Gobi Desert, white blossoms scatter like snow over the thousands of acres of this borderless waste. This is when Second Sis and other middle-aged women, along with young men and women from the village and this piece of earth, take the train several days and nights from Henan to Kashgar in Xinjiang or to some immense field elsewhere, gnawing on steamed buns and pickles, drinking untreated water, and sweating profusely, getting up before dawn to pick cotton for the farm owners. My sister, her peers, and their children willingly accepted this work, no different from what slaves did in bygone centuries. When cotton season ended half a month later, they'd leave Xinjiang and return to our village, skinny as twigs, their faces reddish-black from the ultraviolet light of the high altitudes, the features of men and women indistinguishable. That's where a thorny issue lies: The women don't have to do this, yet they feel they have no choice.

What force compels them to stride boldly, of their own free will, into this self-made otherness?

Money!

Possessions!

Material desires!

Yesteryear's fading sense of national idealism is now completely gone. Instead, we have the individual and their house, their yard, the kitchen with a fridge, the washing machine by the doorway, the couch and air-conditioning in the living room, the home computer on the desk, whether it gets used or not, the tangle of cables, chargers, and extension cords. Things you can see and touch, replacing history as an unstoppable force, the drip-drip of each item, each possession inducing men to leave home in search of work, then luring or commanding women to do the same. It's material desire that's guiding these men and women. I've always thought that in today's China, the greatest force for change in society is the tornado created by everyone's lust for material goods. "Times have changed. Anything a man can do, a woman can do too." The great force that was unleashed with the liberation of women didn't rest as the times changed but unhesitatingly leapt headlong into the next era. And so, completely voluntarily, women took on the duty and responsibility of this new "labor force," knowingly throwing their otherness into any place, any field where a man could earn money. Thus history discards the idea that humanity is divided into two binary sexes, deliberately letting it sink into oblivion.

6.

The contemporary writer Dai Jinhua could be said to have an advanced understanding of many issues. In *Yesterday's Island*, her collection of film essays, she talks about the fate of the women of China after liberation in "Contemporary Chinese Women May Be Less Fortunate Than Hua Mulan," and states with utter clarity: "But this time, the arrival of liberation did not mean—or at least did not only mean—that the new women would enjoy freedom and happiness; rather, it meant they ought to unreservedly offer their newly freed minds and bodies to their liberators and rescuers: the Communist Party and the enterprise of communism and socialism. The only path open to them was to go from being slaves to being people (women), to being warriors. It was not as women, but as warriors that they would attain the same status and equality with men."

This analysis and conclusion concerns the female question in Chinese literature and film but could equally be applied to the lives of rural women in the New China. The women in my clan and on our piece of earth didn't go to war, weren't part of the history of revolution, didn't get any kind of systematic education, yet they too were grains of sand or clumps of soil amid the earth and bore the full brunt of the sandstorm-like assaults and duress of the various movements of the New China. In these books and films, "the only path open to them was to go from being slaves to being people (women), to being warriors," while my family and other women on this piece of earth found themselves forced to go from being old people (female) to new people (women), and hence workers (providers of labor). In other words, they didn't attain personhood so that they, as women, could enjoy freedom and equality with men, but rather they were workers, turning themselves into supermen, into laborers, taking on duties and responsibilities identical to those of their male counterparts while maintaining their previous domestic roles.

In the course of this transformation, they accepted their otherness. This was the beginning, middle, and end goal of the construction of a new category of womanhood.

During this process, whether with Beauvoir's assertion that "one is not born, but rather becomes, woman," which led to the theory distinguishing biological and societally constructed gender, or Fouque's counter that "there are two sexes," or Judith Butler's query in *Undoing Gender*—"But must the framework for thinking about sexual difference be binary for this feminine multiplicity to emerge? Why can't the framework for sexual difference itself move beyond binarity into multiplicity?"—as well as Butler's convoluted deconstruction of identity in *Gender Trouble*—"The task here is not to celebrate each and every new possibility *qua* possibility, but to redescribe those possibilities that *already* exist, but which exist within cultural domains designated as culturally unintelligible and impossible" (what a tangle of words)—none of these, the limited number of books on feminism and women's rights that I managed to read, felt applicable to my clan and the women or womankind living on this piece of earth.[8]

In *Unbearable Weight: Feminism, Western Culture, and the Body*, Susan Bordo says, "My argument here is a plea, not for censorship, but for recognition of the social contexts and consequences of images from popular culture, consequences that are frequently effaced in postmodern and other celebrations of 'resistant' elements in these images."[9] These words are well worth considering and valuing. She talks about "Western culture and the body," but what about our Eastern culture and the body? I personally don't like the story or characters (bodies) of "Hua Mulan Joins the Army." There's an inherent distaste and revulsion for "women becoming men," which isn't about the narrow binary of "women are women and men are men," but because the story doesn't engage with the awkwardness and confusion of Mulan having to live surrounded by men, so we never learn of the unease and anxiety of a female(-bodied) person living in a man's world. The female body disappears from the narrative. "She buys a fine steed in East Market, a saddle in West Market, a bridle in South Market, a whip in North Market."[10] With these purchases, she goes from "daughter" to "warrior." "She parts from her parents at dawn and camps by the Yellow River at dusk. She does not hear her parents calling for their daughter, only the rushing of the river. She parts from the Yellow River at dawn and reaches the Black Mount at dusk.

She does not hear her parents calling for their daughter, only the barbarians riding through the Swallow Hills." The verse moves crisply along, like a shooting star passing through the sky above a battlefield, while the female body vanishes amid the blades and stallions of a man's world. "I open my east chamber, I sit in my west chamber. Remove my battle garb, resume my former clothes. At the window I tidy my hair; before the mirror I powder my face." Thus femininity returns to her. The lyrics tease and manipulate the listener, so the (female) daughter is merely a noun, a symbol. If she did not tidy her hair at the window and powder her face at the mirror, would anyone truly believe that Hua Mulan was not male but female?

In any case, Hua Mulan is the best-known archetype of the "woman-man" in Chinese culture. From there we had other examples, such as Fan Lihua, Mu Guiying, and Dowager She, as well as Qiu Jin, Xiang Jingyu, Liu Hulan, Sister Jiang, Zhao Yiman, and many others. After the establishment of the New China, we had "model female workers," then reform and opening up came with "superwomen." This string of "man-like" heroines, female generals and revolutionaries, ensure that the "woman-man" continues to be the valiant lifeblood of Chinese culture that flows through our soil in all directions. "This abstract, unsituated, disembodied freedom, I have argued in this essay, glorifies itself only through the effacement of the material praxis of people's lives, the normalizing power of cultural images, and the continuing social realities of dominance and subordination."[11] What a convoluted sentence. Why not simply say "effacing the reality of women's lives, equalizing the standards by which men and women exist in the world"? Wouldn't that be clearer? And more certain? That's the clarity and certainty with which our society deals with women. It can't be denied that women of my mother's generation displayed an essential "manliness" as they played their part in the building of socialist society. But in our current historical moment, their daughters and daughters-in-law feel "it doesn't have to be this way, but it's impossible not to be this way." The latter are aware that under the equality that gives them the same "labor rights" as men, they are willingly accepting the incursion and transformation of the new category, turning themselves into "builders" and "laborers" in Chinese society. At the end of the day, the new archetype of womanhood is a Chinese village woman—particularly one from my clan, on that vast, deep soil of the Central Plains, where women are radiant, possessing a unique quality unlike anywhere else in China, or any other country.

7
The Women

A Shocking Feminist Murder

Was the sunlight a few years ago the same as it is today? Or the wind, the sky, the hills, the streets full of people? Trees wither in early winter. Time tramps over the rooftops, and all kinds of other footprints make my hometown feel weary and shriveled. Even that morning, on market day, the sun seemed listless and sluggish, ready to go back to bed, unsteady on its feet and faintly anxious.

Everyone was on edge, waiting for something to happen.

Then, something happened.

A fancy new bus arrived from Luoyang, ferrying a dozen or so foreigners who'd arrived on the high-speed train from Beijing and caught this express bus after some rest and refreshment. Many townspeople were used to seeing foreigners in Luoyang, Zhengzhou, or Beijing, while traveling or working away from home, so they no longer felt the need to gawk. Even so, not once in thousands of years had so many foreigners come to our little town in the Western

Central Plains. Twelve or thirteen of them. Accompanied by two women who must have been their interpreters. The bus parked on the street. They got off and headed west, all jabbering curiously in their strange voices, leaving the interpreters as flustered as mothers needing to feed a dozen kids at once. And still no one knew why they'd come all this way, until the incident happened, and an investigating force several times larger than the visiting group arrived in the town, whereupon we all went, "Oh!" Before that, we had no idea what they were doing here, what they wanted to see and understand, what we had that was worth looking at. Maybe they were just bored? Beneath the noontime sun that early winter day, when the market was at its busiest, unease shrouded us. Those who wanted to sell but found no buyers got frustrated, while those who wanted to buy but couldn't find what they were looking for grew agitated. Everyone was mad at everyone else, and desperation bloomed in all our hearts. Then there were the foreigners, strangers in a strange land. They were attracted by a woman selling garlic by the side of the road. By a girl in a crimson embroidered jacket. By some seven- or eight-year-old kids pissing by the side of the road. By a young woman arguing with a man over whether an egg was fresh or not. Maybe she shouted something nasty at him. Possibly he yelled back at her. Then he gave her a vicious shove.

The woman fell to the ground.

The crowd surged over.

The foreigners joined the crowd.

What happened next was unexpected and uncontrollable, like water breaching a dam and gushing everywhere at once.

People and more people. A crowd beyond a crowd. All the marketgoers rushing to the intersection. They surrounded the young guy who'd pushed the woman. Then the villagers, the townspeople, every single individual on that piece of earth was clamoring and besieging the dozen foreigners. They wanted the foreigners to speak up for the young woman and talk some sense into the young man. Discussion gave way to argument. At this point, the Chinese were one family, and the foreigners were another family. Even the young woman started berating them: Why are you getting involved in our business? One of the foreigners, a man with an aquiline nose, took the opportunity to jab at the young woman's chest and touch her face, saying something no one could understand. Someone punched the foreign man in the face, knocking him to the ground. The crowd started hitting him. They got carried away, and next thing they knew he was dead. His girlfriend, who'd grinned stupidly as her boyfriend harassed the young woman, got beaten to death too. The other foreigners—mostly French and American, mostly women—as well as their Chinese interpreters, were also left battered and bleeding, their clothes torn, clumps of their hair ripped out.

Afterward, when the investigating teams arrived from Luoyang, Zhengzhou, Beijing, and so on, we learned that this international incident in a northern Chinese village had left two dead and nine injured, ranging from the relatively light (thirteen stitches at Luoyang People's Hospital) to the more serious (seven broken ribs). One had a concussion and skull fracture from someone grabbing their golden hair and smashing their head into the concrete pavement. They were sent to a hospital back in the US but were never able to speak again.

The first example of someone losing the power of speech without being left in a vegetative state.

The news arrived that the man who'd been beaten to death was the French philosopher and literary theorist Jean-Paul Sartre (complete nonsense, obviously), and the woman was his lover Simone de Beauvoir (ridiculous, utterly ridiculous). As for the person who lost the power of speech, why, that was a Yale philosopher and UC Berkeley professor of gender studies whose works included *Gender Trouble*, *Bodies That Matter*, *Undoing Gender*, and *Subjects of Desire: Hegelian Reflections in Twentieth-Century France*. (As if!) The other victims included French psychoanalyst and feminist scholar Antoinette Fouque; leading French feminist Simone Veil; French feminist theorist, author, and lesbian and women's studies representative Monique Wittig; and American cutting-edge scholar of the body Susan Bordo, as well as Bengal-born Amartya Sen, Austrian Melanie Klein, and other feminists and women's studies scholars from Japan, Korea, Indonesia, and China. They were all here for a conference in Beijing held in conjunction with International Women's Day, as scholars or representatives of their institutions. (Sartre was there as Beauvoir's plus-one.) Afterward, they came to my Henan village as part of a "study of women's issues in northern Chinese villages" and triggered a shocking feminist murder case. So my hometown got labeled "a shameful stain on international feminism," like a swarm of bees getting besmirched by the blood and shit smeared on the ground.

Zhao Yamin

Head southwest from our village, and after nine kilometers of mountain roads, you come to a place called Fallen Well. Its name dates back to 1640, in the late Ming dynasty, when the dashing King Li Zicheng was retreating after a defeat in battle. When he passed by here, with the sun blazing down and everyone's throats afire with thirst, he spotted an old well in this abandoned village, a pitch-black shaft with a faint glimmer down below: the last dregs of water. But how could they get it out? In desperation, the king yanked the well from the ground and wrenched the shaft onto its side, and the water slowly trickled out. The king and his troops were able to slake their thirst and set off again. Eventually, they overthrew the Ming dynasty.

From then on, this village was known as "Fallen Well."

A few years ago, a young woman lived here: Zhao Yamin, aged twenty-four and a half, plump and beautiful, fond of wearing a red sweater and trousers the color of the moon. She was known around these parts for her hobby of collecting watches. Old-style Shanghai watches made in China, cheap digital watches in funky designs from Hong Kong, and out-of-date "Formosa" watches from a Taiwanese collaboration with some foreign brand. When the police took her away, they found ninety-nine watches in the wooden chest by her bed. The most expensive was a Swiss watch that had stopped working many times, previously owned by a retired department head who'd worn it for twenty-seven years. Half its plating had worn away, revealing the copper underneath; an expert in the county seat assessed that it was worth more because of its age: 22,000 yuan. The young woman had wrapped this costly watch in red satin, stuffed it into a leather case the size of a fist, and stored it in her varnished paulownia wood trunk.

They arrested Zhao Yamin in the back room of a suburban hair salon, after she was reported to the police during one of their anti-crime campaigns. She was naked at the time, sitting with a man on the edge of the bed. They hadn't yet done the deed and were still negotiating her fee. She wanted the watch he was wearing, but the man insisted on cash, because his wife gave him the watch for their wedding. Zhao Yamin didn't care about its sentimental value; she turned tricks for watches, not money. As soon as she'd amassed a hundred watches, she wouldn't take a single client more, not if you beat her to death. No, she'd go home, work in the fields, marry a nice man, have a child, and live a good life.

"Why watches?" all her johns asked.

"None of your business!" she always replied.

At this point, her clients would exaggerate the worth and origin of their watches, claiming that handing them over would be a big loss. She'd ask each man what brand his watch was, how much he'd bought it for, and how long he'd had it, then using her ever-growing knowledge and experience, she'd decide whether or not that was worth selling her body for. Even if it wasn't, she'd do it anyway if she liked the watch. For a particularly expensive specimen, she'd let the man do it twice or stay the night.

Her base price was 400 yuan per session.

To get her hands on that scuffed Swiss watch, she had to sleep with the retired department head for an entire month.

All she wanted was to get a hundred watches before washing her hands of the whole business and living out her days as a married woman in Fallen Well. She'd worked as a shampoo girl at this salon for two years. In her wooden chest, she had ninety-nine watches waiting for her to go back home, a reformed character in a blissful marriage. Sunflowers in the front garden, a vegetable patch out back with greens, cucumbers, and tomatoes. Her husband would water the plants and build trellises for them. She'd bring him cooled boiled water, tipping it into his mouth to make him laugh. When he'd drunk his fill, they'd look around contentedly. The day before, she'd gone back to Fallen Well and put her ninety-seventh, ninety-eighth, and ninety-ninth watches into the chest, all neatly labeled. Then that morning, she'd come back to the salon. At four in the afternoon, she cut the middle-aged man's hair before their romp. While they were still discussing payment, the door to the inner room was kicked open and two cops barged in screaming, "Freeze! Don't move!" As if either of them could have been armed.

They were taken away.

The patrol car was filthy. For some reason, vomit from some drunk hadn't been cleaned away.

She was interrogated in another little room. Her face looked yellow and waxen in the harsh light, suffused with embarrassment. After an awkward silence, she told the interrogating cop and the woman taking notes something truly unbelievable: The reason she was so bent on selling her body for a hundred watches was that the man she loved, someone from her village, had adored watches since he was a child, yet at the age of twenty-two (he was two years younger than her), he hadn't managed to buy a single one. He worked every job he could find and saved up, but then his mother fell ill and he was back to square one. He tried farming instead, but when he'd saved enough money, it was his father's turn to get sick and die in hospital. It was starting to feel as if he'd never own a watch in this lifetime.

She loved him like he was her own little brother.

She wanted to give him a hundred watches.

On their wedding night, she planned to hang a hundred watches from the wall, surrounding the "double happiness" paper cutting. She was just one short. The following month, the ninth day of the lunar calendar, had been chosen as the auspicious date for their wedding. Just seventeen days away. The cop asked her, "Does your fiancé know you're a prostitute?"

"No."

"Does he know you were planning to give him a hundred watches?"

"No. I wanted to give him a surprise he'd never forget."

They sentenced her to three years for prostitution and sent her to a reform center more than fifty kilometers from our county. Her boyfriend went to see her twice a month. After this young man, just as plump as she was, finally agreed to let me accompany him to "Red Light Labor Camp," sixty kilometers from my home, I first stopped by Fallen Well to look at the well: burbling with water, rising from the ground at a thirty-degree angle. How could this round brick shaft with this gleaming mossy surface have been dug at such an angle? How could Li Zicheng possibly have wrenched an entire well shaft on its side to get at the water? When I saw Zhao Yamin, I planned to ask her, "Do you know how anyone could pull a well shaft sideways when it was dug straight down?"

If she said no, I would tell her, "I don't know either. We don't even understand each other; how could anyone hope to understand a well?"

Tong Gaizhi

Less than five kilometers directly east from my home, across a river, is a village called Qiaodong, or East Bridge, so small it couldn't contain a full-throated shout. Over a hundred people in twenty-some courtyard homes, scattered like old clothes at the foot of a hill. One woman from this village was determined to run off with another man, and her husband and son simply couldn't persuade her to stay. The husband promised he'd give up his mining work in Tanzania. He'd leave all his stuff in Tanzania and never stray from East Bridge again. She said it wasn't about that. When she was with this other man, her "heart burst with happiness," whereas she no longer felt happy when she was with her husband.

"Our kid is twelve years old!" he said, as if to remind her.

"I know," she said. "I'm thirty-three, and if I don't try to live a few happy days now, I'll have no time left."

"We'll be able to build a bigger house next year." He was always trying to tie the house to her future. "Once that's done, we'll live better than anyone else in East Bridge."

She didn't care about the future, not with the present spreading before her like gold and jewels. "Is it going to be as nice as the houses in the province seat? The best lives in this village aren't going to be nearly as good as lives in Zhengzhou, are they?"

He had nothing to say to that.

Zhengzhou, the province seat, called to her like the sunrise. She sat across from him, holding their twelve-year-old son, and talked about it like the coming of spring, when all living things would be renewed. On her face was a pallid, awkward determination, and at the end of each sentence the corner of her mouth would twitch. Her husband was five years older than she was, thirty-eight but looking forty-eight. For several years he'd been on an overseas work team put together by the local government. Fixing bridges, constructing buildings, digging mines, and logging. In the course of these jobs, he'd been to more than twenty cities in countries all over Africa. He claimed the best of them, Nairobi, was not as good as Luoyang. "If they're so great," he said, "they wouldn't need us to build their bridges, tar their roads, dig their mines." After five years of hard labor, his face was deeply tanned, and his aging features resembled those of the ebony sculptures of old men you see in shops in China. He'd arrived home three days before, after getting three phone calls from her two and a half months ago. The first time she urged him to come back, he said his plane ticket would cost enough to pay for a wall's worth of bricks. The second time, he said, "What's the point of coming home, wasn't I just home last year?" The third time she called, she was in their courtyard at dusk, and he was at a mining site a hundred kilometers from Dar es Salaam, five hours behind her, with the noontime sun pouring down on his head like fire. "If you don't come home right now, don't you dare say I have no conscience, don't you ever call me shameless. If I'm not here when you get back, don't come looking for me." For two months after that, she didn't call him. When he tried to reach her, her phone would jump around the table ringing, but she never bothered to answer. With her silence, she implored him to hurry home so they could get a divorce, so she could finally put her cards down and say what she had to say.

He came back more than two months after their final phone call.

How come he got the call in summer, but didn't return till autumn? First, he thought she'd only summoned him home because a woman will miss her man, but if she just put up with it the feeling would pass. Second, he hadn't even finished high school and had no idea how to navigate all those airports on his own. One of the company's foremen, a college grad, happened to be going home then, and so he tagged along. But when he stepped through their front gate and set his luggage on the bench, she stood in the doorway and just glared at him. No "Oh, you're back." Unlike in past years, she didn't take his luggage and hurry to get him a basin of water to wash his face or a much-needed drink. She watched as he walked across the courtyard. He put down his suitcase and said, "I'm parched, fetch me some water." She stared at him as if his sudden arrival had startled her, as if he was a stranger who'd blundered into the wrong house. After some hesitation, she got him the water. He guzzled it, set down the glass, and turned to find her back at the doorway. That's when she told him, "I've met someone."

He blinked at her, as if he hadn't heard clearly.

"A Zhengzhou man." She sounded very calm, as if she

were merely relating an incident from last market day. "Let me tell you, I've thought a lot about this, and I'm going to marry him. I wanted you to come back so we could get divorced. Let me marry him." He just looked at her as if he had no idea what was going on, as if *she* were the stranger who'd wandered into the wrong house. A conversation between two strangers. Three months ago, she said, she went to town on market day and somehow or other got talking to this man. He'd come from Zhengzhou as a salesman for his family's business, hawking over a hundred tons of steel rebar and triangular beams. When he was done talking business, he checked into a local hotel and popped out to buy some fruit. There she was, just downstairs, selling summer peaches from the garden. He bought some and struck up a conversation. She followed him up to his suite. The next day, after taking their kid to school, she went back to his hotel. On day three, he didn't go back to Zhengzhou as planned, and she was in his suite again. They were still together, and she wanted to divorce her husband and marry him. When she said this, her husband leapt up ready to smack her across the face, but his trousers caught on a nail and ripped right open. A gust of cold air hit him in the ass, freezing him in place.

"How old is he?"

"Maybe twenty years older than me?"

"That's old enough to be your father!"

"So call him daddy. I like him, and that's that."

It came to him that he should grab a piece of wood and take a swing at her, but when he looked around for one, his eyes lit instead on his secondhand suitcase, full of things for her and their son: clothes, gifts, a soft, white lambskin rug that would go on their bed in the winter, snug as an electric blanket.

"Aren't you ashamed?"

"This is nothing. This sort of thing happens everywhere these days."

"Our son is old enough to know what's going on. Aren't you afraid he'll hate you for the rest of his life?"

She hugged their son closer to her and studied his face, which was calm and placid. She felt guilt for what she was doing to the boy's father, and some other emotion she couldn't name. She'd already done her share of raising the kid, she said. If her husband insisted, she would tear herself away and leave him here. If he really cared about the boy, though, she hoped he'd let her take their son to Zhengzhou. The schools there were much better than anything around here, after all. The other man had agreed to treat him like his own son.

Her husband shot her a vicious look and spat at her feet. That was the strongest response he could muster. Fine, he said, she could go. "Get out of here!" In fact, the sooner the better. It was already dark, though, so she said she'd leave in the morning. She made him dinner, did his laundry for the last time, and spent the evening tidying the house as it had never been tidied before. Then he went to bed in one room, and she and their son slept in another. After the boy had fallen asleep, she crept over to his bed and said, "Aren't you going to beat me?" He stirred but didn't speak. "We haven't seen each other for a year," she said. "If you still want me, I can spend one last night in your bed."

Everyone in my hometown knows what Tong Gaizhi did. For a very long time, this salacious story alleviated the boredom and monotony of our lives. When I heard this story, I sought out her husband, Wu Chengmin, and had to sit with him in his courtyard for a long time before he opened up to me. Next time I was in Zhengzhou, he said, I should look up his wife Tong Gaizhi. If she wasn't doing well, I should tell her to come back to him. They'd been married, after all, and their son still missed his mom all the time. He could go to Zhengzhou himself, but he was afraid that when they came face to face, he wouldn't know what to say. Not finding the right words was holding him back. One year passed, then two, and then it had been a whole three years and he still hadn't made the trip to Zhengzhou. In early March this year, I badgered a friend at the province's TV station until he helped me track down Tong Gaizhi at a Zhengzhou hospital, where she worked as a nurse. I took her for a meal after work, and she told me she'd separated from the older man. Not because he was older, but because he'd lied to her—he was actually still married. Even so, she bore him no grudge. They'd had two happy years together, and when they parted he bought her an apartment, where she now lived with another nurse from her hospital. He was also married with children, but they were together for the moment.

"Don't you want to go back to East Bridge?" I asked. "Don't you miss your husband and son?"

She thought about it for a moment, then shook her head. Smiling awkwardly, she said, "I don't care if you laugh at me or if you write about this: I was married to Wu Chengmin for over a decade, and I never knew what an orgasm was. I had my first one aged thirty-three in the hotel room with the Zhengzhou man. And now I'm with this guy, and we love doing it every single day."

Now I was the one with nothing to say.

It seemed her fate was guided by the bright light of these climaxes. Yet high point or low, east or west, up or down, we all end up walking the same road, and her ending was waiting up ahead for her. I already knew how her story would conclude, but I didn't know what to say. I stared at Tong Gaizhi as she sat beneath the window of the small restaurant, turning visibly paler. Eventually, she surfaced from her silence and looked at me. "Someone who gets divorced because of ... that sort of thing, and still lives on this earth—do you think that person can be human?"

I had no idea how to answer her, but I felt a strange jolt of understanding and appreciation.

"Because of all that, for the sake of those orgasms, I have no regrets even now that I've ended up here."

I kept staring at her, thinking how unexpected it was that such a forward-thinking woman, so ahead of her time, could exist in my hometown. She wasn't attractive, and the medicinal reek of the hospital clung to her, yet no matter what, she had a woman's perceptiveness and acuity about the world. On the piece of earth I come from, this detachment and brightness truly set her apart from everyone else.

Yang Cui

In the summer of 2018, a river in my hometown flooded. When the waters retreated, a dead body was found near a couple of abandoned waterfront buildings. The police investigated these two buildings upstream from the reservoir, dilapidated from the ravages of time, the changing seasons, and the water that had surged chaotically through them, strewing them with weeds, scrap wood, and plastic bags, as if they'd gathered in piles while seeking freedom but ultimately could not find the exit. The deceased had been buried between the two buildings. After the flood, a rotting arm reached from the earth, terrifying a courting couple. First the county cops, and then the city's corpse-removal unit, and finally investigators from the province seat all came to our town.

The body belonged to a woman named Yang Cui, aged fifty-seven and three months, murdered by her son, Ma Xiaofei. After his matricide, Ma Xiaofei went to Shenzhen in search of work. When the police brought him back, he said very politely to the officer, "Thank you for arresting me." The interrogation was as straightforward as inserting a key into a lock—on the trip back, the killer candidly recounted how and why he'd done what he did, an emotional tale that made perfect sense, and even the arresting officer shed a tear for him. It turned out that thirty-three years ago, Yang Cui had been seeing a man from the city called Guan Zhengpeng, even though Mr. Guan had a wife and daughter (yes, another one of those). He kept mentioning divorce, but nothing came of it. Then Yang Cui got pregnant with his child and had no choice but to hastily fall into marriage with her current husband in Shannan, Ma Chuanzi—a full ten years older than she was, an honest, hardworking man of few words. Two months after their wedding, Ma Xiaofei was born. Obviously, Ma Chuanzi knew this wasn't his son, yet he treated the boy like his own. Sometimes people in the village would call the boy a bastard, and Ma Chuanzi would get into a fight with them. By contrast, his relationship with Yang Cui was neither good nor bad.

"It might be that my mother's heart was with that first man all along."

This one line from the dozens of pages that make up Ma Xiaofei's confession contains the hidden foundation of this murder. No one can understand a woman who parts with one man and lives with another for thirty-three years, while holding the first man in her heart the entire time. She never gave her heart to her husband. If the first man hadn't fallen ill and ended up in hospital, and if the news hadn't reached the ears of Yang Cui—who was no longer twenty-four—then nothing would have happened. Life is a pool of stagnant water, unmoving till the wind blows or a sufficiently large rock splashes in. Everything in the world that could be termed life will inevitably get swept up in the ripples. And so, thirty-three years after they parted, news arrived that Guan Zhengpeng was gravely ill in hospital. In his delirium, the name that kept rising to his lips was Yang Cui's. Now fifty-seven, she snuck away to the county hospital. As for what they did during this encounter, what they said to each other, that's a matter of speculation and imagination. In any case, she came home transformed. Everything felt different. While cooking, she scattered MSG into the rice pot as if it were salt. She tossed the vegetable leaves in the garbage and stir-fried the roots. Worse, she couldn't get to sleep and sat all night in the courtyard weeping. After half a month of suffering, she wanted to go back to the county hospital to see her lover, and when her husband forbade her to go, they argued. Ma Chuanzi, now sixty-seven, smacked her twice across the face and shoved her into the bedframe, cracking one of her ribs.

Ultimately, she asked her husband for a divorce.

Naturally, Ma Chuanzi refused. They'd been together thirty-three years, which was as long as their son had been in the world. Their grandchildren were five and eight. How could they get divorced just like that? They quarreled more, hurling plates and pans like they were frisbees. Finally, in the middle of the night, Ma Xiaofei was woken by his mother, who wanted to talk about the divorce. Without hesitation, he took his father's side and told his mother to go back to bed. The next day, she didn't say a single word and neither cooked nor ate any food. The day after that, she remained silent as death. After lunch, there was nothing she could say with her husband at home within earshot, so she took her son down to the river, but they kept passing people they knew from the village, so they headed to an abandoned millhouse a kilometer upstream. The buildings had been gutted, and even the millstone and the bricks around it had been taken away by the villagers for their own homes. Apart from a few older folks, no one knew these two dilapidated buildings had once been a mill. And here, between these buildings on the brink of collapse, mother and son found the silence and solitude they needed. She told him that because his adoptive father wouldn't give her a divorce, she was planning to run off with her former lover. The doctors said Guan Zhengpeng's brain tumor was serious, but he remained in good spirits and could easily live another three to five years. His wife had passed away two years previously, and his daughter was married and studying in Shijiazhuang, Hebei. She was the only one left who could take care of him. Clearly the heavens had arranged for her to be with him in these final years. That's why she needed a divorce. If not, she wouldn't be able to marry him, which would mean she wouldn't be "with" him for these few years, they'd only be "shacking up"—a completely different prospect. A marriage license was needed before they could be called a family. She'd just be having an affair, and all her acquaintances and Guan Zhengpeng's neighbors would say she wasn't human, that she was less than a pig or a dog. Ma Xiaofei's adoptive father would rather die than give her a divorce, and now she was unable to sleep at night. She'd lost more than ten pounds in half a month. When she thought of her first lover, Guan Zhengpeng, she wished she could fly directly to his bedside. Now, she said, her mind had cleared. As soon as he got a little better, the two of them would flee into the hills and find a deserted place to live in. But Guan's year in hospital had drained his savings and used up so much of his daughter's money that she no longer answered his calls. The only solution, she said, was for her son to give her half or more of his 100,000 yuan in savings, which she could use to pay the rest of the hospital bills and find a pleasant hillside home. She knew her son would never agree, which left only one other way to put an end to this: Let her die. That way, she could stop yearning for her lover, and Ma Chuanzi couldn't beat her up again. Also, her son would no longer be tormented by these problems of money and reputation, and he could stop being torn between his biological and adoptive fathers. Yes, she said, she'd made up her mind to die. Xiaofei had two choices: Give her 80,000 yuan and allow her to spend a few years with the love of her life, or strangle her on this deserted riverbank and never think about this wretched business again. With that, she pulled a phone charger from her pocket, knelt at her son's feet, wrapped the meter-long cord around her neck, and handed the ends to him. She shot him a look that said, "Your move." In a panic, her son clutched at her and kept saying, "Don't do this, Mom! Don't do this!"

Then she spoke the crucial words: "Xiaofei, you know Guan Zhengpeng is your real father. Give me the money!"

He made his decision.

He stayed still for a moment, turning it over in his mind, then he hardened his heart. He strangled his mother, dragged her body into the mill, sat on her corpse, and smoked a cigarette. When it got dark, he went back to the village for a shovel and buried her in a corner.

The next day, he moved to Shenzhen with his wife and son and started looking for work there.

Two years after that, the flood dislodged her decomposing arm, which startled the courting couple into calling the police. On the train back from Shenzhen, Xiaofei's anguish made him spew out what he'd done and why, a full confession. At the trial, they put Ma Chuanzi on the stand and asked why he hadn't gone looking for his wife, who'd been missing for two years. "I thought she'd gone to be with her ex," he said. Now that everything was out in the open, a police officer quietly told Ma Xiaofei, "When Guan Zhengpeng heard that your mother had died, he passed away the next day in hospital. If only you'd known how this would play out, you ought to have given her the cash and let her be with your birth dad, while you stayed with your adoptive one. That would have been perfect. Look how things turned out instead."

Xiaofei stared at the officer's solemn face and nodded, expressionless. Then when he said goodbye to his adoptive father, he hugged him with handcuffed arms and said, "Dad, thank you for being so good to me in this life. After the firing squad shoots me dead, bury me kneeling next to my mom."

Wang Pingping

Wang Pingping was finally caught twelve years—forty-eight whole seasons—after killing her husband and burying his corpse. The whole thing—locating the body, reporting the crime, solving the case—was like something from a cheap novel. Her sixty-eight-year-old mother-in-law dreamt that her son, who'd been missing for twelve years, was buried beneath their kitchen floor, and she went to the police station in town to make a report. The police were obliged to investigate every case as a matter of protocol, even if it was just a formality, let alone when it involved an old woman whose son had been missing a dozen years. An officer came to her kitchen and started banging the concrete floor, a space of less than ten square meters, with a wooden pole. When he heard the echo of a hollow space, his ears perked up. He told the onlookers that he hadn't found anything, locked the kitchen door, and went back to the station.

At noon, a police car showed up with four officers in it. They dug up the cement floor and found the missing man's bones and shirt buttons, and the soles of his leather shoes that hadn't quite rotted away. They asked her who'd poured the concrete, and she said it was her daughter-in-law. About twelve years ago, the daughter-in-law was cooking but kept spilling water, turning the dirt floor into mud. She'd gone out and bought some cement, lugged back some sand from the riverbank, mixed the concrete, and spread it on the kitchen floor. Next, they asked the old woman when her son went missing, and she said he'd often disappear for days at a time—he was fond of drinking and gambling. A few days before her daughter-in-law poured the concrete, he had gone out and never came home. The two women spent a few days searching the gambling dens in the town and county seat, but he was nowhere to be found, so they gave up and came back home.

After a while, they stopped looking.

The daughter-in-law started spending more time at her parents' home.

Eventually, she married another man.

The new husband came from very far away, and the old woman had no idea where she was living these days. She said she'd always assumed her son had gone out to play cards or gotten up to some other unsavory business and ended up dead when something went wrong. She could never have imagined he was buried under her own kitchen. For twelve years, she'd cooked and eaten all her meals here, sometimes squatting on the floor. To think she'd been atop her son's head and body the whole time.

"My son was murdered. He couldn't bear the injustice, and that's why he came to me in a dream, to tell me where he was buried," she kept repeating through her sobs to the police officers and other villagers. Her face was dripping wet to start with, but she was so old that her tears soon ran dry.

Half a month later, the daughter-in-law, Wang Pingping, was brought back from a distant county up in the hills of Nanyang. She'd been not quite thirty at the time of her husband's death, and now she was in her forties. Twelve years before, she was four foot eleven, and though she'd gotten older, she remained the same height. Short and dark skinned with thinning hair, she had a round face and regular features, and couldn't be called ugly. Our local cops worked with their Nanyang counterparts to scour the hills till they found her; she was cooking while her nine-year-old daughter did her homework, and her six-year-old son sat in the kitchen doorway watching his sister. There was another daughter, three and a half years old, sitting on the kitchen floor tugging at her sleeve. She was seven months pregnant, and number four was thrashing around inside her, making her belly swell fit to burst. Then the police suddenly showed up in the courtyard of her tile-roofed home, and as the neighbors crowded round to gawk, they charged into the kitchen and said, "Is your name Wang Pingping?"

"Yes."

"Come with us, we have some questions for you."

Startled, she blurted out, "Where are you taking me? I haven't finished cooking. My kids are waiting for their dinner." As they dragged her away, she struggled and cried out, "What is it? What's so important it can't wait for me to finish cooking?"

One of the officers couldn't contain himself and snapped, insinuatingly, "Wasn't your first husband Liu Yigou from the next village to yours?"

She seemed to suddenly remember something. Her face went pale, and sweat poured from her forehead like rain. Without a word, she obediently followed the police out of the kitchen. Biting her lip, she hugged her terrified son and daughters, glanced at her uncomprehending husband, and slowly walked out the front gate. They took her away. Everyone remembered how, eighteen years prior, when she was twenty-three, she'd married Liu Yigou from Heying village four kilometers from her home. She knew she was marrying him because he was attractive and almost six feet tall, but she couldn't quite understand why tall, handsome Liu Yigou wanted her. After the wedding, she gradually realized that her husband had a reputation in his village as an inveterate gambler and thief. Worse, he insisted that rather than living with them, his mother should get her own place across the street. Without his mother there, it was easy for him to stay out getting up to no good with other women. He'd come home roaring drunk and beat up his wife for no reason. If she oversalted the food, he'd smack her across the face. If he called her a couple of times and she didn't answer, he'd fling something at her head, a shoe or a brick. Domestic violence engulfed her like a thunderstorm. What left her even more ashamed and terrorized was that her husband would sometimes bring a nameless woman home and sleep with her in their bed. He'd send Pingping to the kitchen to make them food. Trying to survive, she told him he was free to do what he liked outside, but to please stop bringing women home.

He kept doing it, and she had to keep cooking for them. On the evening of June 21, twelve years ago, he brought back a massage girl from a salon in town. As they got busy in bed, he called his wife over and told her to watch, so she could learn the massage girl's positions and techniques. After the girl left, he drank some more, then ordered her to service him in bed like the girl had.

When she refused, he beat her again.

With one smack, he knocked out three of her teeth so blood spurted from her mouth. That made her want to kill him. This bloodlust was like opening the floodgates: no way to shut them again with water pouring through, and no way to make the water go back behind the dam. She transformed into an alluring, biddable creature, willing to serve him however he wished to be served. If he wanted a drink, she made him some food to go with it. If he didn't, she'd ask if he was sure he didn't fancy a drop. After a few days of this, his verdict was, "This is more like it!" On June 27, when she'd finished laying her plot and gathering her courage, he got drunk again and kicked her for forgetting to salt his fried cucumbers. That kick was like his body's final twitch before death. He asked for water when he was done drinking, and she gave him a cup of pale yellow liquid that ensured he would never wake up again. His dead body, all 110 kilograms of it, lay beneath a pile of firewood in a corner of the kitchen for an entire day, before this tiny woman, weighing just 45 kilograms, buried him beneath the concrete as she'd planned. When the police asked her why the kitchen and not the courtyard or inner room, or even outside the village, she replied, "He was too heavy for me to move, so I had to bury him where he lay." She'd put DDT in his tea and masked the taste with sugar. He came into the kitchen just as she had finished making the poison.

"Didn't you know DDT is already sweet?" asked the officer.

"No, and I didn't dare to taste it myself."

"Did he die right away?"

"It took a while. At first he complained of a pain in his guts, then he was about to say something else, but he passed out instead."

"Why was he in the kitchen?"

"He was thirsty and kept calling for water, then when I took too long to answer he came in to get it himself. I was just about to bring out his drink when he came in."

"Did he say anything before drinking it?"

"He said, 'Didn't you hear me, you sow?' Then I handed him the cup."

His mother moved back in a few days after her son went missing. She often dreamt of her son after that, but it took twelve years for the dream to come that cracked the case and led to Wang Pingping being held in the county jail. The mother-in-law and the police were certain whose body it was, but they still went through DNA testing and analyzed the poison in the bones before they could scientifically confirm that Wang Pingping was the killer. At the police station, the old woman faced Wang Pingping through a grilled window and said, "You went away for more than ten years and never came back to see me. If you'd visited just once, I wouldn't have said a word even if I dreamt of my son dying in the kitchen." Wang Pingping said nothing at first, then as her mother-in-law was preparing to leave, she let out a sad smile. "I had three kids, and I'm pregnant with a fourth," she said. "When would I have had time to visit?" She stopped to think for a moment. "And there's one more thing to clear up—it wasn't me who couldn't have kids. It's your family that has a problem."

And that's how this case of husband murder ended.

A month after this, Wang Pingping was released. She was giving birth soon, and she maintained that the deceased hadn't just beaten her, he'd been vicious in all kinds of other ways. So they reduced her sentence to several years of home surveillance.

None of us thought of this as a sentence. It was more like the powers that be had opened their eyes and had seen what was going on.

Wu Zhimin

Wu Zhimin was one of the very few gay people from my hometown. After getting married to a man, she found that she couldn't stand sharing a bed with her husband instead of her "best friend." Her husband was standing in the way of her love, so she killed him. None of us could understand it. We thought scandals like this only happened in places like Beijing or Shanghai, Guangzhou or Shenzhen, not on our little patch of earth. I heard about this when a friend who hosted a show on Henan TV's legal news channel told me about an "unusual case." When I first heard she was a local, I was stunned. Imagine this kind of thing happening in my own backyard! Less than three weeks later, I was interviewing her at the provincial women's jail, on a hill thirty kilometers from Zhengzhou. We drove through a wooded area till we saw a high wall with sentries; behind it were buildings of various heights, living quarters, a workroom, cafeteria, field (where they took their breaks), and visiting area. Just like prisons in the movies or on TV. Though the air here was much better than in Zhengzhou or Beijing, and the sky was bluer too, because they built the prison where the Yellow River slowly rises, virtually at the top of a hill. The TV station had a close working relationship with the jail, and getting in wasn't much harder than dropping in on a neighbor. After driving up there, making a phone call, parking, showing our documents and registering, we were given some bottled water and led to the visiting area, gawking at everything around us. No wire mesh separated us from the inmates; the visiting area was a couple of rooms guarded by a sentry on the second floor of a three-story building. The four of us—me, the TV host, a propaganda officer from the justice department, and the deputy head of the prison, whom his subordinates called "deputy head" or just "prison chief"—sat around a table large enough that we could have played ping-pong on it. The October sun poured through the glass and wire mesh of the window, leaving striped shadows across the ground like lines of ink. Wu Zhimin was brought in, handcuffed, by an armed guard who nodded at his boss before leaving. We all looked at this murderer who'd smashed her husband's head in with seven hammer blows while he was sleeping. The others seemed to find her unexceptional, whereas my eyes opened wide and my mouth gaped open. She was not yet thirty, tall, sallow, and short-haired. Her mouth and nose didn't seem to match her beautiful eyes, as if they belonged to someone else and had only taken up temporary residence on her face, as if it wasn't her parents who'd jammed this flat nose and wide mouth beneath her eyes. She looked statuesque at five foot seven, and a little plump beneath her white uniform. The serial number on her chest was 328, a good number. She stared back at us before speaking in her West Henan dialect, "Hello everyone. Ask me anything and I'll answer." Her taking the initiative with such frankness put a mysterious smile on the officers' faces, as if they were taking credit. Only I was startled and uncomprehending. The justice department officer, whom the deputy had placed across the table from me, stood up as if she were ready to leave. "No need to put on a show. Do as you're told, and your sentence might be reduced. This is the best opportunity you're going to get." Wu Zhimin nodded at the hulking deputy and hid her cuffed hands under the table. When I sneaked a peek, I noticed her cuffs looked worn, as if many people had had them on before, the metal coating scuffed to reveal a whitish-yellow surface below, the color of a long day fading into evening. I looked at her handcuffs, then at the deputy's face. Did he understand I was asking if we could remove her cuffs? He shook his head no, then he left too. Now it was just me and the people in charge of propaganda and other words.

After another silence, an unforgettable interview began.

"We come from the same place: My home is less than an hour by car from yours. I was surprised that such a thing could happen in a rural village." That was my opening gambit.

She gave me an odd look, then swiftly adjusted herself back into the role of "criminal." A pale smile rose to her lips. "What would you like to know?"

"How … how did you discover … that you liked women and not men?"

"I'll start at the beginning, like I always do." She glanced at the justice official on her right and seemed to receive permission to continue. "When I was little, I didn't like going to school with boys or playing with them. I thought that was just how all girls felt. Then in middle school, most of the girls in my class claimed to hate boys but seemed to enjoy spending time with the ones they liked. Later, working in the fields or going to the market, I noticed girls liked being with guys because they could help carry things and so on. But I didn't want any man or boy to be my partner. I wanted to work with other women. Especially if they were taller and broader than me, and around my age. There's a saying in my village, 'man and woman united, work and never get tired.' Many women giggle when they hear this, because it feels like flirting. Me, I shiver. I imagine a man's hand groping and creeping across my body. I want to be with women no matter what I'm doing. In high school, when a girl started dating a boy, her dorm-mates would keep asking her what first love felt like and so on, and if she wouldn't say, everyone would push her onto the bed and shove her or tickle her until she blurted out something like, 'Holding hands feels like an electric shock,' or 'When we kiss on the lips I feel dizzy.' Then the other girls wanted to know exactly what this electric shock or dizziness felt like. Someday they would try it for themselves. They also liked to distribute the boys in our class among themselves: You have that one, she can have this other one. Then they'd laugh and fantasize about those boys, while I was left cold. When would they allocate a girl to me? The thought scared me! But once I'd had the idea, it grew in my mind like a stalk of grass, like a tree. It grew bigger and taller. Then I reached the final year.

"I was at a boarding school. Three days after New Year, it snowed and the world turned white. It was really cold that night. The girl in the bunk above me was called Liu Yaling. She said her blanket was thin and she was so cold, could she come sleep with me? She climbed down. As she slipped under my covers, I felt strange all over, like something itchy was crawling on me. Her hand brushed against my chest, maybe on purpose, maybe not. A shiver went through my whole body, and I understood what my classmates meant by 'electric shock' and 'dizzy.' I felt as if the bed would collapse if I moved an inch. I lay there perfectly still, then once again her hand lightly touched my, you know, my nipple. I started sweating all over, and threw myself at her ...

"After that night, the two of us spent every night under the same blanket. In the winter, we used the cold as an excuse. When it got warmer, we'd start the night in our own beds, but at some point she would climb down to me or I would join her on the upper bunk. Our dorms at Third County High School had four people per room, two sets of upper and lower bunks. Liu Yaling and I were afraid our roommates would see us being "friendly," and we became wary about getting too close whenever they were around. Then as soon as we were alone, we wished we were tied together. Bound together never to be parted. Maybe everyone was busy doing homework and studying for exams, but no one noticed we were a couple. Then everyone was busy preparing for college entrance exams. Yaling got into Zhengzhou University. I ought to have gotten into Zhengzhou or Henan University, but around that time, I'd started to feel that I loved Yaling more than she loved me, and maybe she might leave me, though I'd never leave her. Distracted, I failed to qualify while everyone around me got a university place.

"Yaling was a city person. Her father was the director-general of our county's forestry bureau. I grew up in a farming village, and my parents didn't know how to do anything but work the land, not even a bit of buying and selling. If I'd been a boy, they'd have allowed me to repeat the year and take the exam again, but because I'm a girl, they said forget it. They'd have given in eventually if I'd insisted, but I didn't insist. I thought even if I went to university, I'd never catch up with Yaling. Her family was from the city and her father was a bureau chief. And a gay relationship—where we were, that would never work.

"When I think about it now, I wish I had repeated the year. If I'd gone to university, I'd have a different fate, and I wouldn't be where I am now. I don't blame Yaling for this, and I don't blame my husband, Peng Daming. I can only blame myself for where I've ended up. When I think about my husband, I feel like death isn't enough punishment for me. I'm so sorry to Peng Daming! Sorry to his whole family. His father and mother are in their sixties, and his mother's sick and bedridden. He's their only son. I didn't just kill one man; I harmed his entire family. We were married for four years, and his parents didn't hurt me in any way."

Wu Zhimin started sobbing. She slumped onto the table and wept so hard she couldn't straighten up. Her handcuffs rattled against the table as her hands shook. The TV host handed her a tissue. I offered her a bottle of water. The propaganda officer shook her shoulder and told her to stop crying and go on speaking. Eventually, she pulled herself together. When she started talking again, she didn't go into as much detail as before and seemed to leave out or understate some things.

"Liu Yaling got into university and then she was gone. Off to Zhengzhou to study. I stayed at home working in the fields. It's like they say, the shrike and the swallow fly in different directions. We were no longer together.

"I didn't see Yaling again after we split up. Didn't hear anything about her. I thought she must have a new friend in Zhengzhou, so I tried meeting someone in my village. I saw three men before I got married, but I wasn't interested in sitting and talking over a meal. One of them seemed okay: an army officer, not bad looking. It's just that he kept trying to hold my hand when no one was looking, and I kept pulling my hand away. Eventually we broke up. No hard feelings.

"I turned twenty-five, then twenty-six. Where I come from, that's considered old. If you're still single then, everyone thinks there's something wrong with you. If only I'd been born in the city. I've heard it's completely fine to be gay there. It's even considered trendy. Some parents even support their gay kids. But in a small village, who would ever dare to come out?

"I got married to Peng Daming the year I turned twenty-seven. He was a good man, an elementary school teacher, and his family owned property and cars. Ordinarily, he'd never have been with someone like me, a woman who's cold toward men, but this was his second marriage—his first wife got a terminal disease soon after they were married, and died a year later. He was thirty-two, five years older than me. We didn't really date; we just met a few times before we got married. Eventually we started doing what men and women do, but I always felt nauseated afterward. I'd get out of bed, throw up in the bathroom, and quietly wash myself. I let him have his way to start with, but then I stopped. Whenever he tried, I would say, 'I'm not ready to have a child.'

"My husband Peng Daming was a good person. He thought I was frigid because I didn't like that he'd been married before, so he treated me extra nicely. He walked almost ten kilometers into town each day for his teaching job, and on the way home he'd buy me something to eat or drink. We'd have been fine if Yaling hadn't shown up. Maybe I'd have gotten pregnant eventually. Then my whole life would have revolved around the baby and I'd forget I liked women, not men. But Liu Yaling reappeared last December, on a Monday. Daming had left for school, and I was busy with something or other when Yaling suddenly came to my home. She was the same as always, tall with short hair and broad shoulders, red cheeks in a grayish face. I was the only one who could see the manliness in her. She wore jeans, running shoes, and a gray Adidas track suit top. People might have thought she was a sports-loving female or woman, but I knew she had no interest in exercise—she just liked athletic gear. She stood at my front gate, staring at me. I don't know how long she was there before I turned my head and saw her. I'd been sweeping the yard. The broom fell out of my hands …

"The early December weather wasn't great. The sky was gray, and it felt like it might rain or snow. Cold but not too cold. We looked at each other for a long time without speaking. Not a single word. After an eternity, she came toward me. I walked past her to shut the gate. Then we stared at each other some more. Tears were pouring down our faces. Still we said nothing. It had been eleven years, and neither of us could think what to say. We both remembered that first time eleven years ago beneath the blanket, and we could have fainted dead on the spot. But the feeling wasn't exactly the same. We'd both gotten married, and we saw things differently from when we were at school.

"After a very long pause, the first thing either of us said—she looked around my courtyard and said, in a quiet voice, 'Are you alone?' I bit my lip and nodded, and she came over to wrap me in her arms …

"If only she hadn't come to me that day. I wish we'd never seen each other again. But eleven years after we split up, she came looking for me. And there we were. That day, I cooked her lunch. After we'd eaten, she told me she got married when she was twenty-seven, same as me. Her husband had a degree in computing and had worked at a few different Zhengzhou firms after graduating. At the time of their wedding, he was a senior executive at a medium-sized company and had bought a flat in the new part of Zhengzhou. She wasn't able to get turned on by him, and he couldn't stand her lack of passion, so they got divorced in less than a year. She said she'd never forgotten me, not for one single day. It's just that she'd thought this sort of thing wasn't possible, so she'd never come looking for me.

"Now she'd thought things through, and if I was willing, I could get divorced too and find a job in Zhengzhou, and we could be together. If I didn't want to be with her, then she'd spend the rest of her life alone, or maybe she'd quit her job and find 'someone else like us' to be adrift with in a big city like Beijing, Shanghai, Shenzhen, or Guangzhou. People there would be more open, and those like us would be not just tolerated but understood.

"That day, she left before my husband got home from school. I walked her all the way to the road outside our village. I was like anyone having an affair, deceiving my husband. When she left, she took my heart with her. We went on in this way, like thieves, for more than half a year. Every month, she'd go from Zhengzhou to the county seat, and I'd visit her. Before returning to Zhengzhou, she'd come to my village too. I even stayed with her twice in Zhengzhou, where she rented an apartment in a housing complex. I stayed a week each time, and my husband eventually found out. As the saying goes, you can't hide fire with paper. He knew I got on well with this high school classmate, but he never understood *how* well. He didn't feel I was betraying him; he just found it bizarre, as if I had some kind of psychological illness. At night, he'd keep asking how two women in bed could, you know ... I mean, he wanted to know how two women could do what men and women do. I didn't tell him anything. I didn't know what to tell him. Last October, Yaling came by again. Her retired parents had gone traveling, and she was taking care of their home while they were away. She wanted me to come stay with her, but my husband refused to let me leave the house. He took leave from the school and stood guard over me, making sure I wouldn't go anywhere. One day passed, then another, then five. Yaling was only going to be there for ten days. We got to day seven, a Friday. My husband finished marking a stack of the homework he'd brought home and dragged me to bed with him. He dropped off right away, but I couldn't get to sleep. My brain was wild, chaotic and swelling and fevered, as if the fire in my mind had singed off my hair and seared my skull. It was the middle of the night and my mind was completely blank, yet something in it was buzzing and hissing. Like I was thinking of nothing at all, like I was thinking of everything. I don't know what time this was, but the detective said it must have been past three in the morning. We'd gone to bed a little after nine. People sleep early when the weather's cold. I'd spent more than six hours thinking of nothing, or maybe I was thinking nonstop about how my husband wouldn't let me go to Yaling. He was the enemy of love. I'd gone off the rails. I was an avenging angel. I got out of bed, found a hammer, and swung it at my husband's head. I don't know how much force I used, and I didn't hear the impact. He didn't make a sound. I didn't count how many times I hit him. I went on the run. When they caught me, the police said it was at least seven blows. I brought the hammer down again and again, and I killed my husband.

"It was awful. I don't dare think about it even now. Blood spattered all over the walls and bed, running like a river …

"I beat my husband to death. I deserve any punishment they give me.

"And now I think—I'd have been fine if I hadn't been born in the countryside. Or if I'd been born in the South, where things are more liberal. Or if I'd insisted on repeating the year and going to university so I could have escaped to a city. If only I were in a big city, where things are more open, nothing would have happened. But I stayed here, on this piece of earth, and I ended up harming Peng Daming, and his parents, and my whole family, and Liu Yaling too. When Yaling heard what I'd done, she quit her job in Zhengzhou and disappeared to God knows where. To this day, I still don't know where she is, and even the police haven't been able to track her down."

Fang Yuhua

So far we've been talking about heartbreak and murder; we ought to look at some other aspects of women's existences.

Fang Yuhua, aged thirty-five, was from my village, though we were in different production brigades. My family lived outside the village limits, while hers was in one of the oldest hutongs near the center, and her family had a new property in the prosperous district near the bus station. Owning a place in this desirable location meant you were high status, well-connected, and wealthy; you could rent it out as a shop or set up a business of your own.

All in all, Fang Yuhua's family's good fortune was like the dawn shining on her destiny, waiting up ahead. Then all of a sudden, just as the wheat was ripening in June, she hanged herself in her family wheat field. At one end of the field was a prolific Lingbao date tree (a special sort of date from

Lingbao, Henan), its trunk about the width of a small plate, its branches stretching out like arms. She hanged herself from one of these branches, with what we called "lasso rope"—a rope that had been slit at one end with a date tree twig and twisted together again, leaving a gap through which the other end could be pulled to make a loop that could contain wheat, hay, or firewood; we used it to tie sheaves of wheat for easy transportation. She pulled the noose around her neck as the June sun beat down from the sky above and spilled across hills and plains and rivers, turning the entire world into a steamer basket, setting everything on fire. The young wheat had been greenish the day before but today was golden and firm. If it wasn't gathered soon, it would fall onto the fields and roadside, ending up in sparrows' bellies. Every village was busy with the harvest. Every household was out in the fields. Fang Yuhua's family owned two fields, a two-mu one to the south of the village, and a four-and-a-half-mu one farther away in the hills to the southwest. The smaller field had already been harvested, and the bigger one was halfway finished. As soon as they were done, they could start threshing. But at noontime that day, she hanged herself from a date tree. Its leaves had been shriveled by the sun into little curls, and the peanut-sized unripe dates were bright green spheres gleaming in the sun. She seemed both prepared and unprepared for this. Prepared because, first thing that morning, she'd brought her daughters, aged six and nine, to her parents' home. Unprepared because, the night before, she'd phoned her husband, who was working in an industrial park in Suzhou, to talk about whether he was coming home for the harvest. Most of the other casual laborers had gone back to their villages, and he was receiving double wages for staying behind. Two times 4,800 yuan. Add that to his per diem and cold weather stipend, and he was clearing 10,000 that month. Think how much grain they could buy with that money, he said. Think how much of their construction costs they could pay off. After doing the math, the couple decided they should do what they'd done in previous years: He would stay in the industrial park while she handled the harvest and threshing and poured the wheat into storage containers, all by herself. Instead, in the middle of the sixth lunar month, just before noon, when she was almost done with the harvest, she rested for a while in the shade of the date tree, then all of a sudden she decided to put her head through a noose.

She killed herself.

She'd had several years of schooling, and before her death she left a note in pencil, the last cry of her heart: "Every day, every year, I work just light [*sic*] a man. But I'm not a man! I see no end to it. I don't want to live."

Actually, she left an unbroken string of words; I added the punctuation. Having written that note, she took her own life.

And so, she died. I read her note again and again. How could Fang Yuhua die? How impossible this life is, yet the waterwheel keeps turning!

Yang Caini

Let's talk about happier things. Something lighter and more hopeful, about the radiant beauty of women's lives on the piece of earth that is my home.

Yang Caini (a pseudonym) is twenty-nine-and-a-half, with an alluring figure, delicate features, and such chic outfits that everyone assumes she must be a fashion model or artist. Five foot eight or so. At a glance, you'd think she might be a dancer or actor, or at least someone who once dreamed of performing on stage. All in all, she is so full of artistic temperament that it sloughs off her if she so much as walks down the street. Italian shoes, Hermès bag, at least two changes of dress, shawl, blouse, or pants each day. No one would ever guess she's from Henan in the Central Plains, where farming is everything, let alone that she's a rural villager. Not only is she from there, but her parents planted crops for a living. I ran into her at a rather swanky dinner organized by the Henan Association in Chaoyang district, Beijing. She was introduced as "a Henan arts worker," which didn't attract much of a response, just smiles and nods. Chinese dinners come with an ocean of etiquette, and no one was going to ask a beautiful, trendy, young woman at the banquet table for her age, occupation, or connection to the other guests. In this borderless sea, attractive women must be kept far from the lighthouses. Naturally, I am familiar with these maritime rules. That evening, however, after an extended encounter with Henan cuisine and Maotai liquor, during which some people collapsed on couches and others made repeated trips to the restroom to pee or throw up, she rose from her place and came over to me. Speaking very softly, she said, "Mr. Yan, we're from the same county."

I was too startled to reply. She said she lived less than twenty kilometers from my home. We were in the north of the county, while she was in the south, in one of the county seat's suburbs. She told me the name of the village, and with a grin, tossed in some dialect only known to people from our county. By the time the big business owners had finished puking, gotten cleaned up, and returned to the table, she was back in her seat.

That's how we met.

Since then, she's been to my home for a meal twice. She's loved singing local opera since she was a kid, and is pretty talented; she even competed in our local TV station's "Pear Garden Spring" talent show. After high school, she got a place at the Central Academy of Drama. She stayed in Beijing after graduating and remains in that glittering sphere. As soon as my wife set eyes on her, she exclaimed, "Do such gorgeous people exist in your county?" Later, my wife and I visited her home, an apartment of eighty-something square meters between the second and third ring roads, in a high-end development that initially sold for over 70,000 yuan per square meter. By now, it's doubled in value. Security was tight—getting in felt like a prison visit. When we reached her place on the eighteenth floor of Block 5, her shoe cabinet startled us both—it was crammed full of at least twenty pairs of high-heeled leather shoes in various shades. My wife told me they were all French and Italian designer brands.

I couldn't pronounce a single one of those brand names, and some of them looked like they'd only be suitable for an exhibition opening or gala performance, which told us what circles she moved in. This made my wife shy and tentative, as if we'd come to see a show but blundered into the actors' dressing room instead. We stood in the doorway for a while in shock, until she told us to take a seat and started making tea, then popped a coffee pod into the machine for us. We sat on an artisanal-looking magenta velvet couch in front of the TV and made small talk for a while. I don't know what my wife said to her, but she led her into the bedroom. As soon as my wife stepped in, I heard her go, "Wow!" Then, "You've got to see this. Get in here!"

And so I was summoned.

The first thing I saw, obviously, was a woman's bed, something no man should spend too much time looking at. The comforter, pillow, sheets, and blanket were neatly arranged and luminously bright, like the pearlescent vividness of a tangle of clouds in the sky with a rainbow passing through it, the sorts of colors you'd only expect to see together in a three-year-old's drawing.

In this multicolored room, designer handbags covered every surface, hanging from the walls, laid out on the shelves and windowsills. Surrounding the tall European-style headboard was an archway of bags, making a pi-shape. The built-in wardrobe on the left-hand side meant no wall space there, but handbags hung from all five of the wardrobe doors. On the right side, they ran down both sides of a window as well as on the sill, making three sides of a square. The top meter or so of the snow-white wall opposite the bed was taken up with four neat rows of bags from all over the world, Prada, Burberry, Dior, Chanel, Louis Vuitton, Hermès, and so on, the cheapest among them costing at least a few thousand, the most expensive as much as 200,000 yuan. Red, black, pale yellow, grayish white, and one with hundreds of colors all jammed together so you couldn't have said what the pattern was. (Later, my wife told me this was an LV City

Steamer.) It had a sunken middle and was made of crocodile skin—I couldn't tell if it was real or fake—and each scale was a different shade, crystalline yellow, bright white, hot pink, darkest black, pure gray, moonlight. A hundred and eighty scales, each a different hue, on a not particularly large handbag, all of them gleaming equally bright, merging together into a sort of pinkish-brown. Every centimeter of the long, thin strap was studded with a diamond—presumably not a real diamond, but definitely not just glass either. This bag was in the second row of the display. My wife stood in front of it for a long while, staring at it, then she picked it up to stroke it. These were Bohemian crystals from Eastern Europe, she informed me. I decided this was surely the priciest of all these specimens. "How much did this cost?" I asked Yang Caini, feeling ignorant. A little bashfully, but also smugly, she explained that this wall of bags would be worth 30 to 40 million yuan—if they were real. Half of them were fake, though. Anything that retailed at over 200,000 yuan was counterfeit. The grayish-white, heart-shaped one right in the middle was a fake Mouawad 1001 Nights Diamond Purse. The real thing would have to be custom-made for a cool $23,190,000. She wouldn't earn enough in this lifetime to buy this bag, she said, and it was even less likely that someone would buy one for her. Still, for years now, she'd been dreaming day and night of owning a real 1001 Nights purse, yearning to receive one as a gift.

That day (which made me think of Zhao Yamin and her hundred watches), Yang Caini served us an old person's favorite dish: fennel dumplings. We left without having asked her what an "arts worker" actually does, nor did we pry into whether she'd bought all those bags or if some had been gifts. Even if only half of them were real, the total cost would still be over 2,800,000 yuan.

Incidentally, Caini is very good to her parents—she bought them an apartment on the south side of the fifth ring road and stays with them every weekend; they always cook her dishes from their hometown.

Zhao Zhizi

I must have a dank, blackened soul. To write this seventh chapter, I spent a lot of time in my hometown, Luoyang, and elsewhere around Henan, excavating the past, going from county to county, village to village, interviewing more than ten women about all kinds of defeats, losses, mundanities, glories, and achievements. The ones I chose to write about are the ones you've just read. A writer's heart is inevitably guided by sensitivity and impulse. I could only write about the women who inspired me. I spoke to a young woman from my village who took a nannying job that a relative found for her in Shanghai ten years ago, and now her Shanghai housekeeping business employs over a hundred people. Not only does she have Shanghai residency, she owns a home in Minhang District. Another woman, Xiaohui, from the hill region fifty kilometers from my home, went to Guangzhou in search of work after graduating from high school, and spent a year and a half tightening screws in a Foxconn factory, followed by a stint at another factory in Dongguan where she lost the tip of one finger; with her own sweat and blood, she eventually worked her way up to become the CEO of a business manufacturing grinding wheels that happen to be essential components of some foreign company's production line. Her accomplishment might not be worth a ton of money, but when she drives back home from Guangzhou, it's in a car worth 3.2 million yuan. She also paid for a paved road through the village, which I've heard cost several million. To be honest, the achievements of these representatives of the female sex would merely be grains of sand in the desert that is China's cities, but on the piece of earth I come from, where we have not yet shed the designation of "national poverty zone," they are a beacon in the dark of night, a road through a barren landscape. If I were a different kind of writer, I could have penned a soaring paean to the glorious women from my hometown, but instead I've lent an ear to the howls of anguish from the weakest among them. Women living a different female fate—the ones walking toward a narrow door, sadly slumping away, gloom rushing toward them.

I don't know Zhao Zhizi's (not her real name) age, appearance, employer, or anything else about her, but when I heard what she'd been through, I was captivated. It wasn't just the ridiculousness that left me gaping at her fate, but also the imaginative space that her life opened up, that tossed me into an infinite chasm. I don't know how long I spent in the abyss of shock, nor how far I traveled past the borders of absurdity. Maybe millions of kilometers. My thoughts were galloping wildly, and I found myself unable to ground these events in any kind of logic or reality.

"Mr. Yan, I'm going to offer you something for your writing: a true story you could never make up."

Permit me not to reveal who said these words to me. In any case, he had a sneer on his face as this tale poured out of him.

"If I sold this story, I bet I could get a couple mill for it, but I'm giving it to you completely free.

"Our protagonist is from Luoyang, like you and me. I know this matter inside out, but I can't introduce you to her. She's called Zhao Zhizi. 'Zhizi' as in cape gardenia. Henan girls don't often have names like Zhizi or Rong'er because we don't have gardenias or banyan trees in our province. Her name made me think one of her parents must be a southerner. When they come up north, southerners are glittering gold, the light in our darkness. We went to the same school, but not at the same time—I'm not sure if she was a few years older or younger than me. And we were in the same line of work, though I'm not going to tell you which TV station she was a presenter at. Anyway, that's what she did, and while working on some program, she got to know a mayor somewhere in our province very well. Not only was she his girlfriend, but she also bore him a son, which meant she was now locked in as his mistress. If that was all, I'd have nothing more to say; I'm not going to get into someone's private business. Obviously everyone's privacy ought to be respected. The problem was, when that anticorruption movement last year tore through the local government, they found that she was *also* the mistress of that city's party secretary and had also given *him* a son. Thank God for that sweeping anticorruption campaign. Without it, we'd never have heard this story. Can you imagine, Mr. Yan? Just think: The mayor knew she was also sleeping with the party secretary and had also given him a son, and the party secretary knew she was also the mayor's girlfriend, and that she'd had the mayor's bastard as well as his own. The mayor and party secretary weren't just love rivals; they were also revolutionary comrades. So that's a contradiction, but it also explains how they were able to get on. Their fates were chained together, forcing them to put up a façade of unity when they were actually rivals. At another level, though, they were truly connected. They had meetings together, they went to the same offices, they worked on the same projects, they were in the same study groups, they made speeches together. Zhao Zhizi, a woman from our town, was inevitably tied to them too, becoming both their greatest wrecker and their most glorious asset. This party committee somehow became completely harmonious and unified, a model for us all. Whether they were working on big projects—reform, investment, or development—or little ones—tearing down or constructing a road, a building, a canal—the committee never, ever fought. Why not? Because they were a family, that's why. Lose and they'd lose it all; win and they'd keep on winning. You know what they fought about instead? Whether this or that kindergarten was better, and which star teacher they ought to transfer to which elementary school, to make sure their sons got the very best education!

"Isn't this story just the dog's bollocks? Can you imagine? Zhao Zhizi was already the mayor's mistress, so how'd she manage to double-dip and nab the party secretary too? And have both their sons? How had she kept it secret at first? How did she tell them? And the men, how did they react? What happened the first time after they knew, and then had to sit in the same meeting room staring at some document? What did their faces look like?

"What time did Zhao Zhizi get together each week with the mayor? What slot did she give the party secretary? After the whole thing blew wide open, how did these men navigate the disciplinary process and court trials? Did they regret what happened, or were they still in love with her?

"Just think, Mr. Yan. Wouldn't this make a fantastic documentary play? Or maybe a film! Could you turn this amazing true story into a novel? It could be a great work about a woman, like *Anna Karenina* or *A Doll's House*. Or maybe it should just be porn.

"Hey, Mr. Yan, why aren't you saying anything? What do you think about this woman from your hometown? Do you pity her? Judge her? Hate her? Admire her? When you mention her in *The Women*, are you going to say she's the brightest light of contemporary womanhood? Is she an opium poppy, or is she a Luoyang peony, our national flower?"

Afterword

Granddaughter

Purple Bamboo Park is at the northeast corner of Purple Bamboo Bridge on the west side of Beijing's third ring road. Purple Bamboo Bridge is at the southwest corner of Beijing's Purple Bamboo Park. I often bring my granddaughter to the park. My granddaughter often brings me to the park too. The buildings look like buildings, the roads look like roads, the pedestrian bridge looks like a pedestrian bridge. We walk past the buildings, down the road, over the pedestrian bridge, and beneath us traffic streams like water. Somehow it feels as if something in the world is still the same, but also not the same. The passing clouds are white, but sometimes they're dark. The setting sun is golden, but sometimes it's murky gray.

The gates of Purple Bamboo Park are always wide open, as if it's simply too exhausting to close and lock a gate.

All types of bamboo line the pathways of the park: purple, jade green, dappled white, bending at the waist toward the path, tugging at the arms and sleeves of passersby. Their leaves stroke our heads as if we're devout worshippers. The bold, vegetal scent lingers in our hair, on our bodies. And maybe it will make us bolder as we look upon the world and quicken our footsteps as we stride down the various pathways of the park, leaving behind all our cares and annoyances.

The pulsing music of group dances echoes through every inch of the park, like Baotu Spring, whose burbling water reaches every corner of Jinan city. You could call it a kind of beauty. You could also call it an annoyance. The ambiguity flows like music. I've heard that some old people get so energized while dancing, they go home and get a divorce. Then they get remarried. My granddaughter and I don't care about all that. Sometimes I watch as she infiltrates the crowd of grandpas and grandmas and dances a few steps with them, then she takes my hand again and we walk on. The lotuses are even prettier than how Zhu Ziqing described them. The willows are taller, more slender and more graceful than in any traditional brush painting.

A rowboat glides sluggishly across the lake like a fat duck.

Mandarin ducks drift along the river like pairs of fallen willow leaves.

My granddaughter's hand feels like a newly hatched little sparrow in mine. Sometimes she takes my finger when we're crossing the road, as a blind person might hold their cane. The world is full of ambiguity; it's also pellucid, jade green. A few years ago, not long after my granddaughter arrived in this world, I was in the ICU of Peking Union Medical College Hospital with a pulmonary embolism, and rubber tubes poked into me like bridges crisscrossing my face and torso. My son and daughter-in-law stood by my bedside, weeping. My daughter-in-law said if I liked, she could bring my month-old granddaughter to visit. I shook my head and muttered, "She's too little. This is a hospital." As I said those words, I realized that my granddaughter wasn't just my granddaughter; she was also my life. My life and death.

After I was discharged, I often took my granddaughter to Purple Bamboo Park in her stroller.

I pushed her along until she started calling me Grandpa.

I pushed her along until she learned to walk.

I know my granddaughter is being raised by her parents and her wider family, but in a hazy kind of way, I feel like she's being brought up by Purple Bamboo Park. When she was one, we brought her to the amusement park here to ride the carousel. When she was two, she went back on the swirling horses. When she was five, she still loved the wooden horses, and the little choo-choo train too. Naturally, after riding, she requires an ice cream. Then she gets hungry and asks for a sausage on a stick or some other snack.

She once said to me, "I love days when I get to ride and eat and drink."

When she was two and a half, we played hide-and-seek in the park, and when we got tired we lay down on a couple of stone benches in the shade of a tree on a slope, looking up at the sky and at Beijing. After much deep thought, she said, "Grandpa, I think we should get married. Then you should stop getting older, and I'll stop growing up, and we can live in Purple Bamboo Park and never go home. We'll live on hot dogs and ice cream. Wouldn't that be great?"

Without a doubt, ideas like this are the most unachievable wishes, true utopias made of lies. Nonetheless, by way of making her a promise, I solemnly nodded.

After I'd nodded, it got dark and we went home.

Time passed, and before I knew it, she was turning three. And then four. Then all of a sudden, five. Time, like the endless streams of people and cars in Beijing, never seems older, yet the roads and bridges age and need to be repaired. Like they always have, and yet always feeling new, the seasons change, and we keep walking hand in hand through Purple Bamboo Park, strolling past bamboo groves, trees, boats on the lake, the amusement park, and we talk about the world, all kinds of things, our marriage. As time passed and she learned about the world and its material conditions, she started saying, "If you want to marry me, you'll have to buy me two ice creams and two sausages." I'd do what she said and the marriage would be on. If I refused, she'd pout, drop my hand, and walk on alone. If I split the difference and only got her one treat, she'd say very sternly, "Fine, we'll get married, but then I'm divorcing you."

This June, the whole family went to Purple Bamboo Park together. As we passed the exercise area, my granddaughter noticed everyone on the parallel bars, rings, or other equipment was even older than me. On one of the medium-height single bars, a man who looked about eighty was doing loops and pull-ups, his wispy white beard fluttering in the air like the wing of a dove. The astonished onlookers applauded him. My granddaughter urged me to have a go, so I obligingly hoisted myself onto the single bar, but when she realized I couldn't do a single somersault, or even a pull-up, she looked so crestfallen you'd have thought the sky had come crashing down. Right there in front of everyone, she said something that would fill us both with despair forevermore: "Is that all you've got, Grandpa? And you still want to marry me?"

With that, she stormed off in disappointed rage, leaving the rest of us to follow her. Her mother quietly told us that two boys in her kindergarten were sweet on her, and were always giving her little gifts, such as chocolates or drawings they'd made in art class. After a startled moment, we had a good laugh about it. Then her father sighed, sadly and selfishly, and said, "My God. What will happen when she's grown?"

That amused the girl's grandmother, whose laughter was like the old people's dance music. We kept walking, past willows, bamboos, lotuses, canals, boats, the amusement park, a teahouse. Everything was ambiguously pretty, just like the changing of seasons, neither spring nor summer, neither autumn nor winter, like a moment from another world. Rowboats slipped between the lotuses, once more like plump, lazy ducks. The mandarin ducks paddled along, once more like floating leaves. The sky was pure white, but with a hint of dirt hidden beneath. The trees were bright green, but every leaf was laden with dust. My granddaughter hopped as she walked, like a bird drifting through the sky with no idea where it's going. After flapping around, the bird worked out where it was and returned to me, dragged me to the side of the road, looked around with a strange expression, and climbed up to whisper in my ear, "We should still get married. When you're old, I'll push you along in a chair, and I bet a lot of people will look at us."

Up ahead of us was a neatly dressed, feeble old couple. The man was in his eighties, maybe close to ninety, looking dignified in his wheelchair. The woman was in her seventies, or maybe past eighty, in a simple crocheted cardigan with a dapper silk scarf around her neck, and her thick silvery hair quivering in the breeze. Her face was flushed with health and her back was very straight. She slowly pushed the wheelchair along the lakeshore, and everyone gave way to them, watching as they passed by. My granddaughter put her hands on my back, mimicking the old lady pushing her husband along.

The waterwheel turns, and all things are possible, as if sunrises, clouds, and rainbows will always be right there among us.